C000041504

Rent Seeking

Rent Seeking

Gordon Tullock

Karl Eller Professor of Economics and Political Science
University of Arizona

The Shaftesbury Papers, 2
Series Editor: Charles K. Rowley

Edward Elgar

© Gordon Tullock 1993

All rights reserved. No part of this publication may be reproduced, stored in a retrieval system, or transmitted in any form or by any means, electronic, mechanical, photocopying, recording, or otherwise without the prior permission of the publisher.

Published by
Edward Elgar Publishing Limited
Gower House
Croft Road
Aldershot
Hants GU11 3HR
England

Edward Elgar Publishing Company
Old Post Road
Brookfield
Vermont 05036
USA

British Library Cataloguing in Publication Data

Tullock, Gordon
    Rent Seeking. – (Shaftesbury Papers)
    I. Title   II. Series
    338.5

Library of Congress Cataloguing in Publication Data

Tullock, Gordon
    Rent seeking/by Gordon Tullock.
        p.   cm. — (The Shaftesbury papers)
    Includes bibliographical references and index.
    1. Rent (Economic theory)   I. Title.   II. Series.
HB401.T793   1993
333.5—dc20   93–28621
                                                                      CIP

ISBN 1 85278 870 4

Printed in Great Britain at the University Press, Cambridge

Contents

Acknowledgements

I am extremely grateful to Charles K. Rowley and Richard E. Wagner, both of whom are Directors of The Locke Institute as well as friends and former colleagues, for providing very thorough and conscientious editorial support that has significantly improved the quality of this book. I am particularly indebted to Charles Rowley who is the overall editor of this series and who, from the outset, helped me to bring together and to organize the body of work on rent seeking which has demanded much of my time since 1967 when I first identified the problem. I am also grateful to The Locke Institute for its efficient secretarial services in connection with the typing of the manuscript.

1. Early Beginnings

One of the first lessons that I learned when I began to study price theory was that the main effects of monopoly were to misallocate resources, to reduce aggregate welfare, and to redistribute income away from consumers in favour of the monopolist. I observed that a significant number of academic economists, both in the United States and elsewhere, devoted much of their time to such issues, analysing a formidable list of monopolistic practices and estimating the degree to which production and distribution were concentrated in the hands of a small number of firms. I further noted that students of monopoly power focused their attention almost exclusively on unregulated private markets. The presumption appeared to be that once government invaded monopolistic markets, whether through regulation or through public ownership, market failures would be rectified.

Such a preoccupation with monopoly in the burgeoning literature of industrial organization during the late 1950s and early 1960s, for me, presented something of a paradox. Perhaps instinctively, or perhaps because of my early price theory training, I shared the prevailing view that monopoly was a significant evil, worthy of the attention that it produced. Yet, I was aware of two widely cited papers (Harberger 1954, 1959) that had determined that the loss of economic welfare caused by monopoly in the United States was very small, perhaps of the order of one-tenth of one per cent of gross national product. Since this conflict between my instinct and my observation eventually triggered my 1967 paper on rent seeking (Tullock 1967b), let me begin this book by revisiting Harberger's contribution.

Harberger defined the loss of economic welfare associated with monopoly as the excess of the loss of consumers' surplus over the gain to the monopolist. The gain to the monopolist was his net profit which, in the constant cost model, is the difference between his price and the competitive price multiplied by the quantity sold at the monopoly price. For purposes of illustration, Harberger assumed that the point elasticity of demand for the industry's product was unity throughout the output range. Figure 1.1 defines the welfare loss from monopoly under these conditions in terms of the shaded triangle (now known as the 'Harberger triangle').

Harberger proceeded to estimate the magnitude of such welfare losses for the United States economy utilizing statistics on

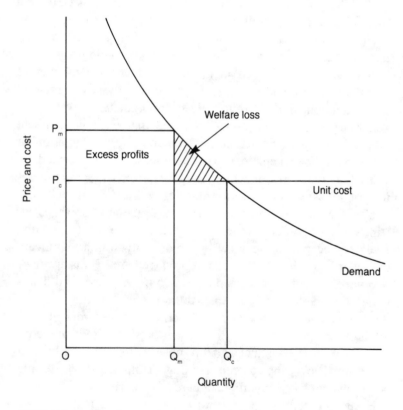

Figure 1.1   Harberger's measure of the welfare loss from monopoly

the rate of return of capital for 73 manufacturing industries for the years 1924 to 1928 compiled by Ralph Epstein (1934). Epstein's study was based on a sample of 2046 corporations accounting for 45 per cent of the sales and capital in manufacturing industry. Harberger calculated that in order to equalize the profit rate in all the industries covered, it would be necessary to transfer $550 million in resources from low-profit to high-profit industries. To take account of total manufacturing, this figure must be augmented to $1.2 billion. On this basis, the resource misallocation in US manufacturing could have been eliminated by a net transfer of 4 per cent of the resources in the manufacturing industry, or 1.5 per cent of the total resources of the economy.

If such a transfer of resources had been effected, by how much would people have been better off? Using Epstein's data, but this time estimating the counterpart of the shaded triangle in Figure 1.1 for each industry, Harberger determined that the total improvement in consumer welfare to be derived with reference to Epstein's sample of firms amounted to $26.5 million. This figure must be augmented for the whole economy to $59 million – less than one-tenth of one per cent of the national income. For a variety of reasons, Harberger concluded that this figure was something of an underestimate and that the correct gain might be slightly in excess of one-tenth of one per cent. Harberger confessed that he was amazed at this result and that he himself had laboured under the delusion that monopoly distortions to the resource structure were much higher than they really were.

Of course, statistics for the 1920s are very sketchy by modern standards and Harberger's assumptions of constant costs and unit demand elasticity are not immune to criticism. Yet, a variety of studies, calculating the welfare loss to monopoly and tariffs in a range of countries (Johnson 1958, Wemelsfelder 1960, Schwartzman 1960) came up with equally minute magnitudes. Let us play around with some numbers to see why this is not really surprising. Suppose that half of the national output is produced in monopolized industries, that the price differential is 20 per cent, and that the average elasticity of demand is 1.5 (Leibenstein 1966). Now the welfare loss to monopoly turns out to be 1.5 per cent. But we used enormous figures to generate this result. Given that private monopoly accounts for a much smaller percentage of national output and that monopoly prices, according to most estimates, appear to be no more than 8 per cent, on the average, above competitive prices, Harberger's results do not seem to be much of an underestimate.

The notion that the social cost of monopoly is approximately captured by the sum of the Harberger triangles remained the conventional wisdom of mainstream neoclassical economics until the mid 1970s, despite well-based challenges by Leibenstein (1966) and by myself (1967). I even taught such orthodoxy myself, though not often since the particular courses for which I was responsible had little need for it. Prior to 1967, I would have taught it without concern had my courses required it. In this respect, I was little different from my fellow economists. In retrospect, it is interesting to note that economics students in general disliked Harberger's result, probably because of their instinctive distrust of monopoly power and of what they perceived to be its adverse implications for income distribution. It turns out that they were right, though for incorrect reasons, and that most professional economists (including myself before 1967), in some cases well into the 1970s, were simply wrong.

2. Leibenstein's Challenge to the Harberger Presumption

The first major challenge to the notion that welfare loss to monopoly is confined to the allocative inefficiencies characterized by Harberger triangles came in 1966 with Harvey Leibenstein's concept of 'X-inefficiency' (Leibenstein 1966). Leibenstein had a great deal of difficulty persuading the editors of the *American Economic Review* to publish this paper and even now it remains a controversial issue among welfare economists. As I shall suggest later, editorial resistance to radically new ideas is a predictable consequence of the organization of economic inquiry (Tullock 1966a). Normal science jealousy guards its carefully cultivated terrain.

Leibenstein acknowledged that the welfare effects of reallocation typically must be relatively small since allocative inefficiency involves only the net marginal effects. The basic assumption of the conventional approach is that every firm purchases and utilizes all its inputs efficiently. What is left is simply the consequences of price and quantity distortions. While some specific price and quantity distortions may be large, it seems unlikely that all relative price distortions would be exceptionally large. However, if firms in fact do not purchase and utilize their inputs efficiently, as a consequence of managerial difficulties, the potential loss of welfare may be many magnitudes greater.

Leibenstein identified three causes of X-inefficiency in firms that are not subjected to high competitive pressures, namely:

1. contracts for labour that are incomplete;
2. production functions that are not completely specified or known; and

3. inputs that are not marketed or, if marketed, are not available on equal terms to all buyers.

(For an explicit model see Crew, Jones-Lee and Rowley 1971.) In such circumstances, the assumption of cost minimization by all firms is simply incorrect. In consequence, firms and economies will not operate on outer-bound production possibility surfaces consistent with their resources. Rather, they actually work on production surfaces that are well within that outer bound:

> This means that for a variety of reasons people and organizations normally work neither as hard nor as effectively as they could. In situations where competitive pressure is light, many people will trade the disutility of greater effort, of search, and the control of other people's activities for the utility of feeling less pressure and of better interpersonal relations. But in situations where competitive pressures are high, and hence the costs of such trades are also high, they will exchange less of the disutility of effort for the utility of freedom from pressure, etc. ... The data suggest that in a great many instances the amount to be gained by increasing allocative efficiency is trivial while the amount to be gained by increasing X-efficiency is frequently significant. (Leibenstein 1966, p. 413)

It is now possible to show the additional welfare losses imposed by monopoly when a shift from competition to monopoly increases production costs by increasing X-inefficiency. Figure 2.1 illustrates two alternative outcomes and is based upon a diagram initially presented by Crew and Rowley (1971). In one interpretation of this diagram, a shift from competition to monopoly increases average (and marginal) cost from C_c to C_m and raises price from C_c to M. Output falls from ON to OZ units. The welfare loss due to allocative inefficiency is depicted by the triangle ADE which is considerably larger than the triangle that Harberger attempted to measure, ABC. To this welfare loss must be added the loss due to X-inefficiency depicted by the rectangle $C_m C_c$ DB which itself typically will be much larger than the loss due to resource misallocation.

In a second interpretation, X-inefficiency manifests itself as an overhead effect and does not strike at marginal cost. In such

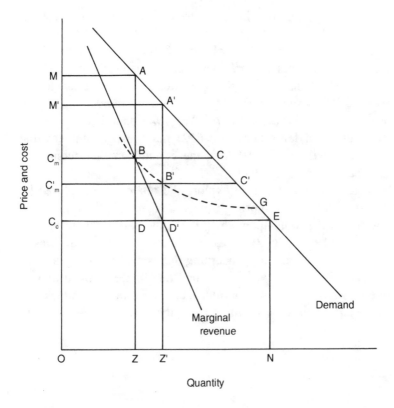

Figure 2.1   The Crew-Rowley model of X-inefficiency welfare losses

circumstances, the monopoly output rate is $OZ' > OZ$ and the monopoly price is $OM' < OM$. Average cost inclusive of over-head X-inefficiency is derived from the rectangular hyperbola constructed through B which cuts demand at G. In this case, the average cost of producing the monopoly output OZ' is OC'_m. In such circumstances, the welfare loss from X-inefficiency is depicted by the rectangle $C'_m C_c D'B'$ which is identical to $C_m C_c DB$ in the first case. The welfare loss due to allocative inefficiency is depicted by the triangle $A'D'E$ which is clearly less than that defined in the first case (Rowley 1973).

On the basis of this kind of analysis, Leibenstein (1966, p. 392) concluded that '(m)icroeconomic theory focusses on allocative efficiency to the exclusion of other types of efficiencies that, in fact, are much more significant in many instances'. Having read Leibenstein's paper, my attention was alerted to the welfare loss issue. I was not convinced by the X-inefficiency argument (see also Stigler 1976). Yet, I was equally not prepared to accept Mundell's (1962, p. 622) pessimistic comment that 'someone will inevitably draw the conclusion that economics has ceased to be important'.

Instead, I determined to explore the other route explored by Mundell, namely 'a thorough theoretical re-examination of the validity of the tools upon which these (welfare loss) studies are founded' (1962, p. 622). I was absolutely certain that the classical economists were not concerning themselves with trifles when they argued against tariffs, and that the US Department of Justice was not dealing with a minuscule problem in its attacks on monopoly. This time, it turned out that my intuition was not misdirected.

3. The Welfare Costs of Tariffs, Monopolies and Theft

As in the case of Leibenstein (1966), the point of departure for my 1967b paper was the conventional welfare loss to monopoly associated with Harberger's famous triangle. Although my article dealt with tariffs and theft as well as with the monopoly problem, I shall draw here entirely on the monopoly example to outline the nature of my contribution, and I shall refer to my original diagram, reproduced here as Figure 3.1.

In Figure 3.1, a competitive industry is assumed to produce output OQ_0 at price OP_0 which is equal to marginal cost, thus generating a total (consumers') surplus depicted by the triangle AP_0C. The monopolist reduces output to OQ_1 and raises price to OP_1, reducing consumers' surplus to AP_1B. According to Harberger, the rectangle P_1BDP_0 depicts a simple transfer of surplus from consumers to monopolist, leaving a net loss of welfare depicted by the triangle BDC.

If the rectangle P_1BDP_0 in Figure 3.1 is the income transfer that a successful monopolist can extort from his customers, surely we would expect potential monopolists, with so large a prize dangling before them, to invest large resources in the activity of monopolizing. Indeed, the capital value, properly discounted for risk, of the monopoly transfer is much greater than the rectangle suggests, since the latter represents only a single period transfer. Entrepreneurs should be willing to invest resources in attempts to form a monopoly until the marginal cost equals the properly discounted marginal return. Potential customers should be interested in preventing the transfer and should be willing to make large investments to that end.

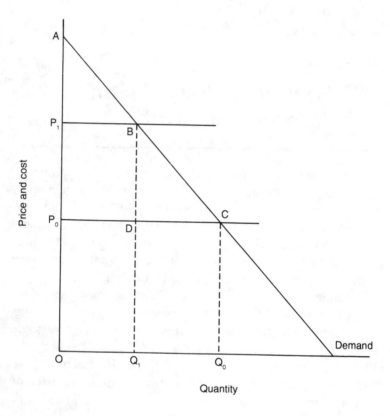

Figure 3.1   Tullock's model of the welfare loss from monopoly

Even when a monopoly is established, continual efforts to break it up or to muscle into it would be predictable, once again involving a considerable investment of scarce resources. Such attacks predictably would induce the monopolist to invest resources in defence of its monopoly powers. The welfare triangle method of measurement ignores these important costs and hence greatly understates the welfare loss of monopoly. Evidently, the 'Tullock rectangle' must be added, in whole or in part, to the 'Harberger triangle' when calculating the potential loss of welfare associated with monopoly.

Although the point that I made in my 1967 article in retrospect was very simple, no one had recognized it before and it was extremely important from the perspective both of formulating policy and of understanding the behaviour of government. The paper eventually made quite an impact on the economics profession. By April 1990, it had been cited 241 times according to The Institute for Scientific Information (Durden, Ellis and Millsaps 1991). Yet, I experienced considerable difficulty in getting it published (Brady and Tollison 1991). First, I submitted it to the *American Economic Review*, where it was rejected by John Gurley, the editor, with the following remarks:

> You will no doubt note that the referee neglects your point regarding the amount of real resources devoted to establishing, promoting, destroying etc., monopolies. However, I have noted it and while I think it is certainly valid, it does not appear significant enough (as a theoretical contribution) to overthrow the referee's recommendation. (16 August 1966)

The paper was also rejected by the *Southern Economic Journal*. Robert E. Gallman, the managing editor, stated that 'Tullock's main point that the "small" triangle does not adequately measure welfare loss in the absence of perfect competition is well understood'. He also argued that I had inadvertently misinterpreted the spirit of Harberger's (1954) paper, and erroneously concluded that '[w]hile Harberger called the small triangle the welfare loss, he also took account of the rectangle but called it, I think, misallocated resources'. (Robert E. Gallman, 6 February 1967.)

If somewhat chastened, I remained unshaken in my insight and submitted the paper yet again, this time to a relatively obscure journal, the *Western Economic Journal*, where it was finally recognized and published in June 1967. Probably because the journal did not circulate widely, my simple idea only slowly penetrated the economics profession, despite my presenting the paper at a number of professional meetings. Interestingly, following my presentation of the paper at George Washington University, I was approached by a member of the audience, Donald

S. Watson, the editor of a widely-circulated book of student readings (Watson 1965), who asked my permission to reprint it in a revised edition. In view of the relative obscurity of the *Western Economic Journal* and the large circulation of Watson's *Book of Readings*, it seems likely that there was a considerable period of time during which my idea was known and understood by first-year economics students, but not known at all by the average professor of economics.

It is interesting to speculate upon why my 1967 paper encountered such inflexible resistance from the leading journals of economics which yet published large numbers of essentially ephemeral and insignificant contributions. I believe that a number of factors played a role, many of which I had anticipated in my 1966 book, *The Organization of Inquiry*, and others that I learned after I embarked on my own editorial career, also in 1966, with the first publication of *Papers on Non-Market Decision Making* (see Rowley 1991).

To understand the behaviour of journal editors, it is necessary to take account of the non-market environment which is central to their operations. The large majority of academic journals are non-profit organizations brokering a 'market' in published scholarship which is made up of individual scholars who themselves are either public employees or employees of non-profit organizations. This is not an environment in which entrepreneurship predictably can thrive. The often unpaid editors of journals no doubt are motivated to do their best to select the most promising articles from among the contributions they receive; but their best may not be all that good. For, as I observed in 1966, 'the job of journal editor, although respectable, is not one of sufficient attraction to get the very best personnel' (Tullock 1966a).

Where editors are respected, but ordinary contributors to the literature in which their journals trade, and where they are unpaid or lowly-paid servants of non-profit journals, they may lack both the skills and incentives to identify the unusual, original articles that cross the editorial desk. They may be attracted more by high technology than by creative scholarship (Rowley 1991). Such a bias will not be countered by reliance upon unpaid anonymous referees who, under the shield of anonymity, are not under any great pressure to reach the correct decision. Both editor and referee have incentives to play safe, to accept high-technology articles that make a marginal contribution to a well-established field, but to deny publication to papers that threaten to pull down the pack of cards of normal science. As I noted in 1966, '[t]he prestige of a journal is affected by the articles it prints; it is not affected by those it turns down. This probably leads the editors to some degree, at any rate, to play safe' (Tullock 1966a, p. 147).

In any event, my 1967 article was simple, low tech and brief, factors that evidently did not enamour it to the editors of two leading economics journals. Random factors in the choice of referees may have played a role. However, I suspect that my experience was not unusual, as Leibenstein's difficulties with the *American Economic Review* tend to confirm. Such inefficiencies may not matter much as long as the journal market remains reasonably competitive. In my case, I suspect that editorial inefficiencies retarded the dissemination of the rent-seeking insight by no more than seven years. Leibenstein, perhaps as a result of greater stubbornness, was able to wear down the editor into revising his initial rejection decision.

4. The Cost of Transfers and Competing for Aid

In 1971, I returned to the theme of my 1967 paper, which as yet had made little headway in mainstream economics. Drawing on my discussion of theft, rather than of tariffs and monopoly, I directed attention to the cost of transfers. The welfare economics literature at that time was awash with notions of interdependent utility functions and of utility-enhancing income redistributions. Governments were accredited with a major role in such transfer processes, allegedly because of the public good characteristics of the charitable motive (Hochman and Rodgers 1969).

The strong implicit assumption in such analysis was that transfers were effected costlessly from rich to poor individuals by impartial and well-advised governments that determined the size and composition of their transfer programmes by reference to the charitable preferences of the rich. Such arguments seemed to me to bear little relationship to the realities of the political process. My paper set out to bring a dash of reality to the redistribution literature (Tullock 1971).

The problem is that, although the actual operation of charitable giving is profitable to all parties, its mere possibility sets off behaviour on the part of all parties, aimed at improving their respective utilities, but wasteful of scarce resources. Suppose that individual T perceives that individual K may make a charitable gift. Under these circumstances, he would be well-advised to invest in becoming a more suitable object of K's charity. In cases with which I am familiar – Chinese beggars – such behaviour may lower the utility of all concerned. When I was in China, occasionally I would see beggars who had deliberately and usually horribly mutilated themselves in order to increase their charitable take. Even though I might be disposed to supply the charity that they sought, I always found that their mutilations inflicted a considerable negative utility on me.

In the Western world, such drastic measures are less frequent. However, many would-be recipients of charity do engage in a certain amount of resource expenditure to improve their receipts. Granted that the potential objects of charity may behave in such a manner, the political donors feel obliged to invest resources in attempting to control such subterfuges. Such interactions are not simply a modern phenomenon. The hiring of almsmongers by medieval princes was an early effort to reduce the wastage of resources in attempts to attract charity by potential beneficiaries of the royal largesse.

The problem worsens sharply when private charity gives way to government redistribution of income. Of course, such government transfers are only in part involuntary. Presumably, tax-payer-citizens are interested in making charitable gifts to other persons; and may choose to use the state as a co-operative instrument for that end. It seems likely, however, that government income redistribution is carried well beyond the point where those who are paying for the redistribution benefit. In my view, perhaps 90 per cent of all income transfers through the state are of this involuntary nature. They are the result of lobbying activities on the part of recipients, combined with ignorance and/or political weakness on the part of those individuals who supply the transfers. Transfers in the form of farm subsidies and of import protection for domestic steel producers and motor car manufacturers clearly fall into this category.

Much more clearly than in 1967, my 1971 paper focused on the resource cost of competitive lobbying of politicians and bureaucrats, both by those who sought to extract government transfers and those who sought to prevent them. One side or the other will win each such battle; but, from the social standpoint, the resources invested in the conflict between the two interest groups are entirely wasted. The fact that the transfer game itself is clearly a negative sum does not imply that those who engage in such political battles are behaving irrationally. It is just one example of a prisoners' dilemma in the oft-times inconvenient world in which we find ourselves.

In 1974, I was prompted by some probing criticisms from Edgar Browning (Browning 1974) to sharpen my 1971 insight and to further segment the government transfer process (Tullock 1974). Browning's commentary focused attention on examples of broad-based tax reform that transferred income from one group of millions of people to another group of similarly large size. With some justice, he claimed that voluntary contributions to lobbying often were not evident as the motive force for such redistributions. This led me to reflect upon the publicness characteristics of certain kinds of income redistribution and the free-riding that such characteristics implied. This phenomenon offered an explanation for the fact that, in democracies, there occurs a very large amount of self-cancelling transfers of income back and forth within the middle-income groups.

One kind of transfer process – the kind that I had earlier outlined – clearly was subject to what I now call Wagner-type lobbying (Wagner 1966), in which politicians respond to well-defined interest groups within their districts and show more interest in brokering benefits to those groups than almost anything else, at immense cost in terms of legislative commitments. The actual effect of this kind of lobbying is far greater than the direct resource costs involved, because a great many people who are not involved in lobbying find themselves affected by the outcome. My 1971 article talked mainly about transfers of this sort: decisions on appropriations or programmes that had a fairly concrete and narrow direct effect for some limited groups of people.

Another kind of transfer, however, involves large numbers of individuals most of whom do not view the effect to be sufficiently large as to justify the investment in lobbying resources. In such circumstances, the outcome is apt to be random. For some such changes they benefit, for some they lose. We might anticipate that, over the population as a whole, individuals who are not involved in active lobbying would tend to gain about as much as they lose. I should add that transfers from the wealthy to the poor do not feature much in this kind of random redistribution.

My 1974 reflections led me to conclude that the population either invests in lobbying or participates in a lottery. For the first group, which is probably small, my original description is more or less correct. For the second, and much larger group, there is an excess burden but, on the average, no net transfer of income or wealth. It is interesting to note that the cost of transfers debate was conducted in *Kyklos* and not in the *American Economic Review* since George H. Borts, the managing editor of the latter journal, had rejected my 1971 paper citing the following referee's remarks:

> This paper does not have anything useful to offer. Its principal point is that the possibility of income or wealth transfers has the unfortunate consequence that people invest resources either to abstain or to prevent them. (George H. Borts, 18 February 1971)

In 1975, I extended my analysis of transfers to demonstrate that wasteful competition over transfers was not restricted to individuals but also occurred among the various levels of government within a multi-layer system. In 'Competing for Aid' (Tullock 1975), I illustrated my thesis by reference to public road rebuilding programmes. I discussed a situation, common in the United States, in which a higher level of government programme provided assistance to lower-level government organizations in accordance with their 'need'. I showed how lower-level organizations would respond to such a set of incentives by deliberately neglecting road repairs in order to qualify for higher-level subsidies. My arguments were not hypothetical. I showed how the city of Blacksburg had deliberately skewed road repair contracts away from its most damaged roads in order to be targeted for repair by the Commonwealth of Virginia. I showed how the development of divided centre, limited access toll highways during the early 1950s was almost completely self-aborted once President Eisenhower introduced the federally-subsidized interstate system.

The local community that allows its road system to deteriorate in order to qualify for state subsidies or that runs down its hospital system in the expectation that the federal government will replace it is in exactly the same situation as the Chinese beggar who mutilates himself to obtain charity from passers-by. In both cases, the action is rational. In both cases, the effect is to lower the welfare of those involved.

5. The Concept of Rent Seeking

The reader will be aware that the term 'rent seeking' was not applied in any of my early contributions to the welfare cost literature. The term was invented in 1974 by Anne Krueger in a paper published in the *American Economic Review* (Krueger 1974). The author was unaware of my contributions to the subject, no doubt because they had been published in relatively obscure journals, and therefore did not cite them in her paper. The fact that her article was published in a major economics journal, together with the catchy nature of her term, 'rent seeking', undoubtedly speeded up the dissemination of the basic idea within the economics profession.

Krueger's article focused attention upon market-orientated economies in which government restrictions upon economic activity are pervasive facts of life. Such restrictions give rise to rents in a variety of forms; and people often compete for rents. Sometimes such competition is perfectly legal. In other instances, rent seeking takes illegal routes, such as bribery, corruption, smuggling and black markets. Krueger developed a model of competitive rent-seeking for the important case when rents originate from quantitative restrictions upon international trade. In this case, she inferred that:

1. competitive rent-seeking leads to the operation of the economy inside its transformation curve
2. the welfare loss associated with quantitative restrictions is unequivocally greater than the loss from the tariff equivalent of those restrictions; and
3. competitive rent-seeking results in a divergence between the private and social costs of certain activities.

She provided estimates of the value of rents from import licences from India and Turkey, finding them to be large relative
to the gross national products of those countries.

It is interesting to speculate as to why Krueger's paper was
accepted by the *American Economic Review* following the journal's rejection of my two earlier articles on an almost identical
theme. It does not seem to me that the intrinsic randomness of
the refereeing process was entirely responsible. I believe that
three factors contributed to the editorial decision. First, Krueger's
paper was somewhat more lengthy and a little more technical
than either of my two papers. Second, the paper contained some
statistical measures, albeit very crude, of the magnitude of rents
involved. Third, and most significant in my judgement, was the
fact that her analysis focused on rent-seeking in India and Turkey, whereas my articles utilized examples clearly relevant to
the United States. Referees tend to be less troubled in recognizing insights that challenge the status quo if such insights appear
to be directed at far distant lands. They become much less com-
fortable when acknowledging that they have been teaching their
students falsehoods that impact directly on an understanding of
their own domestic economies. In any event, Anne Krueger's
forceful and well-written article served an invaluable purpose in
publicizing the basic idea of rent seeking widely across the
English-speaking economics profession.

It is perhaps noteworthy that three early contributors to the
rent-seeking literature – myself, Anne Krueger and Jagdish
Bhagwati (Bhagwati 1980; Bhagwati *et al.* 1984) – have all
spent a good deal of time in the Far East, where there coexists a
number of immensely successful cultures capable of generating
high-quality art, literature, etc. Yet, many of these civilizations,
despite their cultural successes, are economically backward, even
though they evidence no shortage of highly-intelligent, well-
educated, and highly-motivated individuals.

The *émigré* Chinese of southeast Asia and the United States
perform extremely well, as do the *émigré* Indians of Africa.
Only in their own homelands do they fail to perform well. The
phenomenon is not peculiar to Chinese, Indian or Islamic cul-

tures, but rather is located in the traditional governmental institutions of these various backward societies. Rent seeking offers a powerful general explanation of this apparent paradox. It is not surprising that our common exposure to economic failure in culturally-advanced societies led Krueger, Bhagwati and myself to the rent-seeking explanation.

It used to be customary in the lumbering industry to cut down the trees, roll them into a stream and float them down to the mill. There was a tendency for some of the tree trunks to get caught in gigantic jams that actually dammed up the waters of the stream. The breaking of these dams, a highly-dangerous activity, involved, at least in myth, the locating of the key log. When the key log was removed, the log jam was broken and the downstream movements of the logs recommenced.

It would appear that the rent-seeking concept was a key log in certain areas of economic research. In these areas, progress was retarded by the existence of such a jam. Once rent seeking was discovered, there followed an immense florescence of research, taking the form of an exponential curve, as relevant ideas began to disseminate throughout economics. Of course, the rent-seeking concept has now found its way well beyond economics into the litany of political science and sociology. It has found its way on to the pages of the *Wall Street Journal* and even into the speeches of better educated members of Congress. Interestingly enough, such congressmen do not appear to be unduly perturbed when they confront the real implications of their professional life.

This rapid intellectual advance has been well-chronicled in two volumes of readings. The first volume – *Toward a Theory of the Rent-Seeking Society* – was edited in 1980 by Buchanan, Tollison and Tullock and contained a large majority of the articles on rent seeking that had been published up to that time. The second volume – *The Political Economy of Rent-Seeking* – edited in 1988 by Rowley, Tollison and Tullock could afford to be a good deal more selective and encompassed a much smaller percentage of the incremental output of papers. The major introduction to the second volume, by Charles Rowley and myself

(Rowley and Tullock 1988), could and did present a much more comprehensive picture, and a better balanced assessment of the research that had been completed up to that point.

On the whole, what has been done since that time has been an extension of the same basic concepts into other areas. The use of resources to obtain through the political process special privileges in which the injury to other people arguably is greater than the gain to the people who obtain rents is now a major subject in economics. It has spread well beyond economics, into political science, orientalism and sociology.

This raises certain problems which require clarification. The first of these is that investing resources in order to obtain a rent is not necessarily rent seeking. For example, if I were to invest resources in research and invent a cure for cancer, which I then were to patent, I should certainly become wealthy on the rents that would be generated. This, however, is not really what we mean by rent seeking. The result of my resource investment is not only that I am better off, but so is almost everyone else.

When I was editor of *Public Choice* I used to receive, on average, twice a year an article by a young assistant professor or sometimes a graduate student who would excitedly point out that research and patents were examples of rent seeking. It is true that resources are invested and that rents are derived, but some activities bear little resemblance to the overall welfare losses that are imposed by the artificial creation of tariff barriers. If, on the other hand, I were to invest resources in obtaining a law prohibiting the import of a newly-devised cure for cancer because I am myself a manufacturer of an older and less effective one, then I might gain, but almost everyone else would lose. This is the kind of thing that we mean by rent seeking.

The second limitation of most of the rent-seeking literature is that it deals with the manipulation of democratic governments in order to obtain rents through injuring other people. The US farm programme is an example. Speaking as the only person in public choice who has actually written a book on dictatorships (Tullock 1987b), I can assure readers that these impositions are not restricted to democracies. Indeed, what is called socialism in much of the backward world is simply an elaborate mechanism for transferring rents to friends and close supporters of the dictator.

It is an unfortunate fact that recent events which signal the death throes of socialism and the rebirth of what is designated as capitalism have not brought about very great improvements from the rent-seeking perspective. In what is called 'crony capitalism', the man who in the past would have been a rather inept manager of a government-owned sugar central is now the owner. He is still inept and still requires special government protection to support his activities. In both cases, typically, he does very well for himself.

Attempts to measure the scope of rent seeking, which will be discussed later, have not led to any definite conclusions. Superficial examination would seem to indicate that rent seeking is much more important in dictatorships than it is in democracies (Tullock 1987b). This book will primarily concern itself with rent seeking where it involves manipulating democratic governments. This is not because democratic governments are particularly prone to rent seeking. It is because most of the research has been done in this area; and, in fact, it is much easier to do research in the relatively open situation of democracies than it is in the murky environment of most dictatorships.

Another restriction is that I shall not write much about rent seeking in the form of private seeking of private monopolies. This is essentially because I do not consider such activities to be economically significant at the present time, though they have been important in the past (Rowley and Tullock 1988). Today it is very difficult indeed for a private group, without government aid, to obtain a monopoly by any method except by providing commodities at low prices and with good-quality service.

This is partly because there are antitrust laws (which in fact sometimes inconveniences companies that are sole producers because they are simply cheaper and better). But more important is the fact that the economy is large, transportation and communication are easy, and almost any monopoly obtaining excess profits is likely to attract competitors. For the most part, private markets are highly contestable. In small corners of society we may still find companies producing some commodity for which the total demand is low enough so that it is unlikely to attract a competitor even though it is selling at wide price-cost margins. But this is the exception and not the general rule.

For the most part, companies do not make the kind of excess profits that they would make if they had a private monopoly. Nor is there much evidence that X-inefficiency raises private costs in allegedly protected markets (but see Franz 1992). As we shall see, publicly-sponsored monopolies also frequently do not make very large profits although the fact that the businessmen, labour unions, and academics seek them out indicates they are certainly better from the owner's standpoint than a purely competitive situation.

For the rest of this book, we shall primarily concern ourselves with the manipulation of democratic governments to obtain special privileges under circumstances where the people injured by these privileges are hurt more than the beneficiary gains. We shall also evaluate the behaviour of individuals who attempt to defend themselves against such monopolies and of people who engage in lobbying activity for the purpose of dismantling them. The latter activity I would not call rent seeking; but there are some people who would.

6. The Political Market in Rent Seeking

As it happens, the rent-seeking research programme, for the most part, has followed the public choice tradition of which my own work is a part. Anne Krueger's paper (1974) has stimulated a separate research programme labelled by Jagdish Bhagwati as 'directly unproductive profit-seeking' (DUP) (Bhagwati 1980). Both programmes focus attention upon individual or group economic behaviour of a rational, self-seeking nature which nevertheless destroys rather than enhances the resources available to society. Both programmes have radically changed our understanding of the behaviour of political and bureaucratic markets and may have shifted the views of many individuals on the value of constitutional constraints. Yet the two approaches differ significantly, most particularly with respect to the role of political markets in the rent-seeking society (Rowley 1988a).

My initial 1967 paper directed the attention of welfare loss scholars away from private and towards publicly-created monopolies and away from Harberger triangles towards Tullock rectangles. But only in one sentence did I hint at the public choice implications of these insights, noting that governments usually do not introduce tariffs in the absence of interest group lobbying in favour of this instrument of trade protection. In retrospect, somewhat surprisingly, I failed to develop this implication as a central feature of my paper, thus delaying the public choice linkage for some four years.

The public choice linkage came in 1971 with my paper on the cost of transfers. I emphasized in that paper that the opportunity to effect wealth transfers through the machinery of government, on at least a partially coercive basis, encourages lobbying and counter-lobbying in a negative sum game as individuals and groups invest resources in attempts to obtain transfers or to resist transfers away from themselves.

The crucial public choice aspect of this insight is the notion that the mere possibility of transfers attracts rent-seeking and rent-protection outlays that will condition the nature of the transfer outcome. More generally, the particular rents made available by government fiat *are determined by and do not determine* the level and composition of rent-seeking outlays. The political process is itself endogenous to the rent-seeking process. In contrast, DUP analyses rent seeking in terms of exogenously determined rents, paying little or no attention to the public choice characteristics of that market. In this book, I emphasize the public choice approach to rent seeking and ignore the DUP approach (though I do rather like the term DUP). In this section, I shall briefly review the principal actors in the political market for rents, the voters, the media, the interest groups, and the bureaucrats. First, I must review the role of those who broker that market in exchange for votes, campaign contributions, and other perquisites of office, namely the politicians at all levels of the federal system.

The Legislators

In the public choice research programme, politicians are modelled as providing a brokering function in the political market for wealth transfers. Special interest groups capable of effective organization 'demand' such transfers. Other more general groups, including many individual voters, incapable of such effective economic organization, 'supply' such transfers, albeit sometimes after an ineffective struggle. Politicians effect political market equilibrium, balancing their own benefits against their costs at the margin, maximizing their individual utilities, variously weighted in terms of expected wealth and expected votes (Rowley, Shughart and Tollison 1987). It is within the framework of this basic model that I shall review the behaviour of United States' legislators. With minor adjustments, the approach applies to democratic legislators worldwide.

Let me start with a quotation from Republican Congressman Armey, who recently proposed an amendment to the Agricultural Act providing that farmers with more than $125 000 a year of non-farm income would not receive any government subsidies. His amendment was defeated 2–1 on the floor of the House of Representatives by a recorded vote. The immediate reaction of someone not schooled in public choice is that two-thirds of the US congressmen had lost their minds. Imagine voting in favour of giving government subsidies to farmers who are so wealthy that their non-farm income exceeds $125 000 a year. Armey, however, explained the matter:

> There are no weak sisters on the agricultural committee. They do what the committees do very well. They spend five years filling their silos with chits and then they call them in.

Anyone paying attention to Congress can think of very many other similar cases. Senator John Warner, a rather conservative legislator from Virginia, for example, for many years succeeded in preventing the Army from closing down a fort which was so antique that it actually had a moat. I am happy to say that it was finally closed down; but only by being converted into a national monument and museum with almost as many employees as the fort had supported.

As one of the co-authors of *The Calculus of Consent* (Buchanan and Tullock 1962), I am not arguing that 'log-rolling' trades of this sort are always rent seeking. Indeed, in many circumstances they actually lead to a better result than would be obtained if no such trade existed. It can however be used, as in the two cases cited above, to generate rents.

Indeed, in some cases, bills without any log-rolling potential at all, but which are clearly of a rent-seeking nature, pass through the legislature. The various legislative expansions of medicare in the US are examples. Here, of course, there is a powerful special interest group in the form of doctors and other medical service providers; however, it seems fairly certain that congressmen are more interested in the very large number of voters who benefit from these services, and who do not realize that they are paying taxes to finance them.

The United States is a particularly convenient place for empirical research in this area because it can be subdivided into the 50 states, 48 of which are contiguous to each other. Although the legislative institutions bear considerable resemblance, they are not identical. The situation is ideal for cross-sectional research, and the very detailed statistical data available make quite elaborate research of this sort possible. McCormick, Tollison and Crain have been especially prolific in researching these issues (Crain and Tollison 1990).

Legislative trades even occur in local government. Recently, a bond issue was defeated in an election vote in Pima County (which includes Tucson). The apparent reason was that the various road-repair projects did not include anything for the southwest district. The city council and the county board of supervisors redrafted it so that there was something for everybody. In this case it is likely to be one of the cases where log-rolling leads to a superior outcome. Each of the individual road repairs would certainly be defeated if voted on all by itself; but the package which will mainly contain road repair and improvements which are indeed socially desirable or at least very close to socially desirable got through.

Thus, this example may not constitute rent seeking, in our definition of that concept, even though there are trades. Legislative trades are not in and of themselves rent seeking or undesirable. It is only when the trades are used to produce wealth-reducing commodities like the farm programme or to maintain useless army posts which are surrounded by moats that the issue comes up.

A particularly striking example of this kind of thing is the decision by the Democratic Party in the US Congress not to push for significant reductions in American defence after the collapse of the Soviet Empire. The explanation given by congressmen in public speeches, and mentioned in all the newspapers, is that the congressmen are worried about losing military bases or contracts to defence industries in their districts. Thus, the real purpose of maintaining the military will not be buying insurance in the event that the Soviets should revert to Cold War strategies, but buying votes in a large number of different congressional districts.

In addition to the more-or-less straightforward cross-section regression studies carried out by Tollison in association with numerous research associates, a number of other scholars have done excellent work. Peltzman (1976) and Stigler (1971) are names that immediately come to mind. Stigler is primarily famous for having been the first person to point out that government regulatory agencies are normally not 'captured' by the people they regulate. Normally what happens is they are set up by the people they regulate. As he once put it, complaining about a regulatory commission protecting the people regulated from falling prices is very much like complaining about dentists because they work on teeth. In both cases they are doing their job. Such regulatory agencies are usually driven by specialized interest groups and are by no means as profitable to the companies that they regulate as some of the literature suggests. One problem, first discussed by Posner (1975), is that these agencies are primarily employed to transfer money back and forth among politically powerful groups.

There is a particularly clear cut example of this. The regulation of telephones by the Federal Communications Commission was largely the result of lobbying by AT&T which was beginning to find competition cutting into its profits. Nevertheless, AT&T was only one, comparatively minor, beneficiary. During the period when the telephones were regulated by the Federal Communication Commission in a centralized way, the price of long-distance calls was kept artificially high in order to subsidize local callers. It was, in essence, a tax on part of the economy in order to subsidize a large number of voters. It is particularly interesting because it is not obvious that the voters who were subsidized actually gained.

The long-distance calls which were held at an artificially high price were partly ordinary citizens' calls, and only partly business calls. Although the poorly-informed voter thought he was getting a subsidy from the business calls, in a competitive economy, even those would eventually be reflected in higher prices of consumer goods. Thus the individual who found a dollar taken off his local phone bill by this subsidy, paid for by high prices on long-distance calls, in all probability would pay a dollar or more per month extra in higher prices on various consumer goods. The regulation generated an invisible tax funding a rather visible subsidy, to the benefit of vote-seeking politicians.

Even this, however, is a little too superficial. It is not at all obvious that most people receiving this subsidy knew that they were receiving it, let alone that they were paying a tax. It was only when rival interests began talking about eliminating it that the real situation became clear to the average voter. Nevertheless, the average voter did want low prices on his local telephone bill, and brought political pressure to bear both on his congressman and on the Commission. He probably failed to realize that there was an offsetting cost.

Peltzman's work has been directly connected with income transfers and he has argued more or less that politically powerful people, essentially in the middle class, have used the government structure to transfer funds from the wealthy to the poor. Actually, to say that they transfer resources from the poor is not literally true. What happens is that the poor do not get very much of the largesse of the welfare state, indeed, probably less than their votes would normally entitle them to (Tullock 1989). It is unfortunately true that both Stigler and Peltzman, prominent economists to say the least, made a fundamental mistake. They talked about the whole process in terms of its welfare transfer outcomes and did not discuss at all the rent-seeking cost of the process.

This is a particularly impressive lacuna in the case of Stigler, who talked about regulatory bodies as being set up for the specific purpose of benefiting the interests that had arranged them, but never discussed the cost of this process. Recognition that such costs exist is of course the heart of rent seeking. Becker, who wrote a very good article on interest group competition

(Becker 1983) in which he pointed out that the result of certain groups pushing for special privileges and other groups counter-pressuring to avoid being victimized should lead to a balance which is at least arguably some kind of political optimum, failed to emphasize the rent-seeking cost of this exercise.

What do congressmen get out of all of this? Since they are engaging in rent seeking they must get something, but I suspect usually not very much. There is talk about campaign contributions and it is true that congressmen can privatize some of the contributions. No doubt this has an important influence on their behaviour; but it is very small compared to the value of the privileges they hand out. It is not the major rent-seeking cost.

More important is the careful courting of the congressmen by lobbyists. The many expense-account restaurants and night clubs found not only in Washington DC but in the state capitals are evidence of that. Once again, however, such outlays are relatively low compared to the value of the gifts that congressmen hand out. The major cost of rent seeking must be found elsewhere. It seems likely from the standpoint of the congressmen that the principal reward they seek out is simply being re-elected. Each pressure group argues strongly that it can sway at least some votes, and provide some campaign monies, and that the congressman had better therefore pay careful attention to its requests.

The congressmen, or for that matter the state representative or even the city council member, is normally convinced that he is vulnerable at the next election and that he must pay careful attention to various small groups of voters. This being so, his staffers spend a great deal of time on such matters. This work is particularly impressive because frequently the congressman represents a number of different groups, each of which wants something and each of which to some extent objects to the requests of other groups. He must forge some cautious compromise in which everybody gets a little something. The net effect of this may be that, for each of these groups, the gain that they receive, minus the cost of all the gifts to the others, is actually modest or even negative, once rent-seeking costs are accounted for.

Thus the bulk of the cost of a specific policy output is not the rent seeking that triggered it but the unsuccessful outlays by other groups that the congressman trades off in order to implement it. Unfortunately, this has so far escaped measurement; and I have no suggestion as to how to make such measurements. The fact that it is difficult to measure does not imply that it is qualitatively insignificant.

The complexity of the various pieces of legislation that now wind their way through the legislature, each of which is normally an immense pastiche of specific provisions dealing with specific problems in accord with the wishes of some small group, is a major cost for the country as a whole. Most of the gigantic volume of laws, and for that matter the even more gigantic volume of regulations, are never read by the nominal decision-makers, or indeed by any single individual inside or outside the legislature. They are closely scrutinized by attorneys seeking to use them for private advantage.

The congressman or the secretary, if it is a regulation, simply does not have the time to read all of this detail and, in addition, he would probably not fully understand it should he do so. The Internal Revenue Act is an informative example. There used to be, before the Reagan reforms, 17 pages in the Internal Revenue Act dealing with the raising of racehorses. This provision had been introduced successfully by lobbyists for the racehorse 'industry' and carefully surveyed by officials from the Internal Revenue Service who wanted to see to it that political revenues were not damaged excessively. It is doubtful whether more than four or five people actually fully understood those pages.

In this case we know that the clauses must have been very favourable for the horse-racing industry because when the Reagan reforms abolished those sections, the racehorse industry immediately experienced a severe economic depression. The price of prime stallions, for example, fell catastrophically. Thus, this was a case in which, quite inconspicuously, a group of very wealthy men, most of whom in fact were pursuing the raising of race-horses as a hobby, obtained very great tax reductions from special interest legislation. The cost of such secretive lobbying, however, is extremely difficult to measure.

It is not at all obvious that the congressman regards the fact that he does not read most of the bills he passes as immoral or the fact that he would not understand them if he did as pitiful. After all, all his colleagues legislate in a similar fashion, and his own lack of attention to detail is protected by the rational ignorance of the electorate.

The cost to society as a whole, however, from this professional ineptitude must be very great indeed. One of the functions of government is to provide a national co-ordinated policy programme. If policy, in fact, is a very large collection of special provisions which are never co-ordinated, or for that matter not even all read by any one person, then this function fails.

One of the duties of the courts is to deal with Acts of Congress that are inconsistent, either internally or with each other. Fortunately for the courts, but unfortunately for each of the rest of us, most of these provisions are simply gifts to individual interest groups and hence they are not strictly speaking inconsistent. They cause difficulty only by raising the federal deficit and increasing regulatory intervention; and the courts are not responsible directly for these outcomes.

One of the characteristics shown by American public opinion polls is that most Americans distrust and dislike Congress but trust and like their own Congress person. This is a fairly clear example of the role of the Congress person in a rent-seeking society. The average American realizes that the whole bundle of bills that I have been describing serves to his disadvantage. He also realizes that his representative is seeing to it that among the large collection of wealth-reducing bills there are a good many which he himself benefits from.

Assume, just for sake of argument, that each congressman in the House of Representatives can influence 1/435th of the total legislation. The individual voter feels that 1/435th is influenced in his favour by the congressman. The other 434/435ths, on the other hand, most likely are to his net disadvantage. Since he cannot influence Congress as a whole, he tends to dislike Con-

gress and yet to like his own congressman. This dichotomy is
entirely rational.

The Voters

The first thing to be said about voters is that typically they are
very badly informed. Any specialist who discusses policy issues
even with well-educated citizens quickly realizes that this is
true. One illustration of this is that public opinion pollsters usually encounter quite appalling ignorance if they choose to question people in detail on almost any issue. For example, should
they ask questions like: 'Which is the fissionable kind of ura-
nium?' they may find something of the order of one-tenth of one
per cent of the population is correctly informed. If they change
to another form of questioning such as: 'Do you feel informed
about atomic energy?' they find that large majorities of those
polled are informed. In political polls they always find that a
significant minority do not know the name of their President.

The majority of voters do not even know the name of their
congressional representative. Louis Harris & Associates have
responded to this ignorance by asking not for the name, but for
the voter's opinion on whether he knows it. Even here they get
only 65 per cent who say they know (*The American Enterprise*,
May/June 1992, p. 102). This lack of information tends to irri-
tate political scientists. Statements like 'You have a duty to cast
an informed vote' are frequently included in American government classes. Perhaps the average voter does have such a duty;
but it is clear that he pays little practical attention to it.

One of the first contributions of public choice to this field was
the demonstration, first by Anthony Downs (1957) and then
elaborated on to some extent by myself (Tullock 1967a), that the
average voter may recognize his civic duty, and may in fact feel
guilty if he does not become well-informed. However, in strict
cost benefit terms he is rational to be ignorant. The reason for
this is simply that the influence his individual vote has on almost
any election is so small that even very modest information costs
swamp expected net benefits from informed voting. Thus, the

average voter makes a correct calculation to remain potentially unaware, even if his Professor of American Government does not approve of his rational calculus. He may even make the correct calculation to avoid the polling booths come election day.

There are, of course, a number of people who are well-informed, and I presume the bulk of the readers of this book will be among them. They are to a large extent people who are pursuing a hobby of politics or, in my case, of international affairs.

With these hobbyists, however, it is notable that political information does not seem to have very much effect on their vote behaviour. Polling information indicates that the more information a person has, the less likely he is to switch from one political party to another. Thus, it would appear that he acquires the information for the purpose of carrying on conversations with other people, feeling superior and, more importantly than either of these, cheering on his team. Baseball used to be more important as a national sport than it is now. Fans then memorized immense volumes of statistics about various baseball teams. They never let that affect the question of which team they supported.

This lack of political information is of very great importance when we speak of rent seeking. Unfortunately, it is not simple straightforward random ignorance. It is biased ignorance. An individual is likely to have a good deal of information about a few narrow subjects which concern him deeply.

A farmer probably knows a good deal about his particular crops and, in general, has been informed by the various agricultural journals he reads about the political programme for those crops and what his congressman has done about it. This is the ideal arrangement for a pressure group since the farmer almost never has much information about other aspects of the overall political programme. For example, a proposal to cut back the acreage of US farmland ultimately may cause starvation in parts of Africa. The agricultural journals will never note the relationship between cause and effect, not least because such a linkage would make their readers feel guilty and they might switch to another publication.

Such biased ignorance is not restricted to farmers. I myself am an academic and have listened to a good many speeches by political candidates of one sort or another directed at academic audiences. Such speeches normally include at least something about the public good aspects of education with the general drift of argument somewhat to the left of centre because that is judged to be what an academic audience wants. Always they include comments about the importance of education, the need to have good teachers, and the need to pay them well.

Name recognition is of great importance in elections. Both professional politicians and political scientists agree that one of the problems of a candidate who is not a current incumbent is simply to get his name recognized. The incumbent usually already has such recognition. The elaborate mailing out of campaign literature, officially listed as information, in the period between elections is to a large extent an effort simply to get voters to recognize the name of their congressman.

To repeat, this information is distributed asymmetrically and is not just the property of the well-established interest groups. Congressmen are fairly continuously approached by people who want a specific favour or some project in their particular area carried out. An important example of this is the complaint by senior citizens that their social security check has not arrived or that the Social Security Administration has made some kind of an error.

In general, in this area it seems likely that congressional intervention makes the citizen service of the Social Security Administration better than it would otherwise be. Whether this improvement in service is worth the cost is something on which, as far as I know, there are no studies; but I would guess that it is cost effective. A large part of any congressman's staff is engaged in tasks rather similar to this and for that matter simply to responding to letters from constituents.

In general, the fact that a congressman says he is on a particular elector's side is pleasurable; but if he does not actually bring home the pork, get whatever favour is requested, he is likely to be remembered for that rather than for his politeness. Most congressmen have a large staff which, in addition to dealing with what we might call the wholesale market, the major pressure groups, also attempts to accumulate votes on a one-for-one basis by taking care of various minor problems.

The question of whether dealing with these minor problems benefits the country as a whole is open; and whether the benefit is worth the cost is an even more difficult question. It should be pointed out that the cost is not just the salaries and other perquisites of office of the congressional staff. As a general rule, most government bureaucracies give any inquiries from a congressional office top priority; and hence, one of the costs of congressional intervention is that many other things, some of which may be more important, are put aside until the office has responded to the congressional inquiry.

The result of all this is that voters are, to a considerable extent, a major source of rent seeking. It should be pointed out, however, that for some types of policy determination a system of direct popular votes or referenda is superior to log-rolling within the legislature. Well-organized pressure groups can frequently manoeuvre the legislature into enacting legislation that would never get through a popular vote.

The countervailing problem is that a direct popular vote puts the issue before a large number of voters, most of whom do not know anything much about the issue, and have at least some tendency to vote either for or against entirely in terms of their confidence in the governmental process. But it is very hard to look at the results of referenda in areas where pressure groups operate without feeling that the referenda do reduce the frequency with which severe costs are imposed.

Yet voters who, let us say, vote against a quota on eggs are often the very same voters who are apt to push the congressman into providing them with special privileges. Only when the subject is so transparent that even the badly-informed voter notices what is going on will referenda tend to drive out special privileges for small minorities.

There is a good deal of talk in the popular press, as well as in public choice literature, about campaign contributions both by individuals and by political action committees (PAC). There is no doubt that these outlays influence congressmen. There is also no doubt that such outlays are very small compared to the value of gifts that congressmen distribute (Tullock 1989). Therefore, it seems fairly certain that the effective pressure exerted on congressmen is not by way of campaign contributions. Indeed, it may well be that the principal reason congressmen are interested in campaign contributions is that the latter are viewed as a good measure of the political influence of the pressure group and hence of the number of vote gains or losses that they can provide.

Thus, the voter is a rather shaky reed upon which to depend if the object is to achieve good government and a government which in particular only spends money on things that are generally worth purchasing. The average voter benefits from the activities of those pressure groups of which he is a member although the benefit may be much smaller than he thinks it is. On the other hand he is injured by all the other pressure groups and the net effect is that he is actually worse off than without any of them. The limits of his information, however, mean that he is actually only able to function effectively by promoting pressure groups. In consequence, the outcome is that there is a good deal more wasteful rent-seeking than there would be if somehow or other people were able to vote in terms of their long-term interest.

Let me conclude this discussion of the relative weakness of voters in the rent-seeking market-place on a more formal note by setting out the model of rational voter abstention and rational voter ignorance on which this judgement rests. I am aware that certain Chicago economists, notably Peltzman (1990), do not accept these models and argue that all voters are fully and rationally informed on political matters. I am aware of no theoretical contribution that they can rely on to overcome the problem defined by the model that I now outline, and which originally is due to Downs (1957) as finessed by Tullock (1967a).

Suppose that an individual is possessed of some political information that leads him to favour the Democratic Party candidate in a particular election (whether for the presidency, for the Senate or for the House of Representatives). The pay-off to the individual from voting in that election is given by the expression

$$BDA - C = P \qquad (6.1)$$

where B = benefit expected to be derived from the success of the individual's favoured candidate, D = probability that the individual's vote will be decisive in the election, A = probability that the individual's political information is accurate, C = cost of voting for the individual and P = pay-off. Certain aspects of this expression merit further discussion. B refers, of course, not to the absolute advantage of having one party or candidate in office, but to the difference between the candidate and his opponent. The factor A is often omitted from models of this kind. It is included here because I wish to consider variations in the amount of information acquired by an individual; and the principal effect of being better informed is that an individual's judgement is more likely to be correct. In essence, A is a subjective variable, which ranges from minus to plus one in value.

The factor D reflects the probability that an individual's vote will make a difference in the election. For a United States presidential election, this probability typically is less than one in ten million. The factor for C is the cost in money, time and inconvenience of registering and voting in an election. For some individuals, this may be negative since they obtain pleasure (perhaps in the sense of relief from the social pressure to vote). If voting is perceived to be an instrumental act, however, then the decision to vote or to abstain will depend on the weighing of costs and benefits as above-outlined.

For most individuals, the cost of registration and voting is probably in excess of $10 and for some, it will exceed $100. For most individuals, the value of the factor ABD, in almost any election, will be less than one cent and for very few will it be more than $1. It follows from this that only those individuals who experience pleasure from voting (i.e. whose valuation of C is zero or negative) should rationally choose to vote. No doubt this explains why fewer than 50 per cent of voters turn out to the polls in US elections, although it does not really explain the sizeable turnouts that do occur, since D remains very high even at the reduced voting levels that are observed. Evidence certainly supports the view that individuals are more likely to vote in close elections (Barzel and Silberberg 1973). Probably those who enjoy politics, and for whom C is negative, are well-represented in the set of active voters.

Even for those who decide to vote, however, it is by no means evident that they will decide to become well-informed. The factor A presumably increases as the quantity and/or the quality of an individual's political information increases; but so does the magnitude of C as the relevant costs of information are added to the cost of voting. Whatever happens to A, its impact is always cushioned by the low value of D which is an inescapable consequence of the indivisibility of political markets. Herein is to be found the crucial weakness of democracy, the principal determinant of the evident bias of the political process in favour of voters who are concentrated and well-informed on issues that are significantly relevant to them and against voters who are dispersed and ill-informed on issues that are less directly relevant. Herein, also, is to be found the reason for the political vacuum into which the special interests penetrate in order to rent-seek, to the general detriment of society as a whole.

The Media

In terms of the model outlined in equation 6.1, let us assume, for each political issue, that the voter is either ignorant, casually informed or well-informed, thus simplifying the reality of a continuous variation across this spectrum. In order to distinguish between these three states of knowledge, it is necessary to analyse the behaviour of the mass media, through which most voters obtain what information they have on political issues. This analysis focuses attention on *the politics of persuasion* and on *the economics of lying* (Tullock 1967a).

Most of the mass media, when they carry any political information at all, combine it with a great deal of other information carefully balanced to reflect the tastes of their respective customers. The typical reader, listener or viewer does not pay equal attention to all items that the media supply, but rather focuses upon those of particular interest, largely tuning out the rest. Moreover, he does not necessarily remember over any significant period of time the information that initially attracts his attention. Even that which is retained may not be given much, if any, serious thought when the voter commits his vote.

At the time of voting, therefore, the individual may be in a state of complete ignorance on many, indeed on most, issues, either because he has not been exposed effectively to the relevant information or because he has not been sufficiently impressed as to retain and/or to make use of such information. Alternatively, he may be aware of the issue and have some amount of factual information about it as the result of essentially casual receipt of information together with an evaluation of that information that led him to remember it. I shall refer to this state as *casually informed,* and this state will be the principal concern of this section on the media. Thirdly, the individual may be extremely knowledgeable about the issue, because its outcome is expected to impact significantly on his utility. In such circumstances, the voter predictably will be impervious to media persuasion or to the lies of politicians, even if he will not always prove capable of forming accurate judgements on the issues concerning which he is well-informed. The well-informed voter is the pressure group voter *par excellence*, a rare yet highly-predictable phenomenon, casting his vote very largely in terms of the particular issues of great interest to him.

The pattern of behaviour which this picture of the information held by voters dictates for the politician essentially is that described by log-rolling. Politicians will follow widely and strongly held opinions, and will promise to confer simple, easily perceived benefits on small groups. They will attempt to disburse the costs of such policies lightly across the rationally ignorant and rationally casually informed electorate. They will attempt to access the mass media in order to influence casually informed voters to vote for their policy platforms. Let me now return to the model defined by equation 6.1 to outline the role played by persuasion in political markets characterized by casually informed voters. Equation 6.2 reflects the new situation:

$$BD_p A - C - C_p = P \qquad (6.2)$$

where C_p is the cost of effort invested in persuasion and D_p is the likely effect of such persuasion on the probability that a voter's vote will be decisive. Even if voting itself has a negative pay-off, efforts to persuade may not, since advocacy is more likely to affect the outcome of an election than is a single vote. Of course, there will be great variation in the magnitude of D_p from person to person. It is important to note that C_p is very small for certain categories of voter. In particular, individuals engaged professionally in providing material for the mass media may be able to insert considerable persuasive effort at almost zero cost.

The stockholders of the mass media will place limits on this process where it threatens to lower the net worth of their stock. If there exists any principal-agent problem, however, management characterized by specific political agendas may invade the mass media specifically to engage in political persuasion, and then will actively encourage propaganda favourable to their causes. This phenomenon is even more characteristic of the class media, which not infrequently exist primarily for the purpose of political advocacy. Teachers, especially those in higher education, are also well-placed to push political agendas at little or no cost to themselves, especially where such views are left-leaning and conform to the politically correct dogmas of the large majority of college administrators.

In communicating in order to persuade, inaccuracy in information is important only if it is likely to be exposed to the targeted recipients. In this respect, media competition plays an important constraining role. In dictatorships, or in environments characterized by media monopoly, false information may exert a powerful influence. Fortunately, the information revolution has significantly weakened the prospects for such manipulation, quite contrary to the expectations of George Orwell and Aldous Huxley.

For the political propagandist of any persuasion it is rational to lie if the anticipated benefits exceed the anticipated costs. From this perspective, important deductions follow. The more expert the recipient, the less beneficial is the lie. The more important the political issue to the recipient, the more likely it is that the lie will be detected. The more frequent the transactions with the recipient, the more costly long-term is the ultimately to be detected lie. All this renders the casually-informed voter extremely vulnerable to lies, especially since there are no stringent laws protecting voters from false advertising by politicians or by the media. In particular, the ability of major newspapers to protect the anonymity of information sources and the increasing difficulty for 'public' personalities to sue newspapers successfully even for gross libel, enable propagandists to manipulate the media as a source of politically productive lies at a relatively low cost.

The Interest Groups

The rationally casually ignorant voter is a very slender reed on which to build the foundations of democratic politics. He is much more likely to be the recipient of the dispersed costs than of the concentrated benefits of the legislative process. He is much more likely to suffer the net costs of random prisoners' dilemmas than to enjoy the systematic gains-from-trade outlined in *The Calculus of Consent* (Buchanan and Tullock 1962). Is it legitimate, in such circumstances, to infer that the forces of supply and demand in political markets are driven not by individual voters but by interest groups; that collective action replaces individual action in the battle over the spoils of politics that is the *raison d'être* of democratic politics? If so, what predictions can be made about the rent-seeking consequences of competition among pressure groups for political influence?

The relatively optimistic, rose-tinted spectacles scenario of interest group competition is that advanced by Gary Becker in two elegant and highly-influential articles (Becker 1983, 1985). In this model, Becker presents a theory of the political redistribution of income and of other public policies that builds on competition among pressure groups for political favours. Active groups produce pressure to raise their political influence, where all influences are jointly determined by the pressures produced by all groups. The political budget equation between the total amount raised in taxes and the total amount available for subsidies implies that the sum of all influences is zero. This itself is seen to have a significant effect on the competition among pressure groups.

Each group is assumed to maximize the income of its members under the Cournot-Nash assumption that additional pressure does not affect political expenditures of other groups. Political equilibrium depends on the efficiency of each group in producing pressure, the effect of additional pressure on their influence, the number of persons in different groups and the deadweight costs of taxes and subsidies.

Efficiency in producing pressure is determined in part by the cost (recognized though not emphasized by Becker) of controlling free-riding among members. Greater control over free-riding raises the optimal pressure by a group and thus increases its subsidy or reduces its taxes. Efficiency is also determined by the size of a group, not only because its size affects free-riding, but also because small groups may not be able to take advantage of scale economies in the production of pressure.

Becker places considerable emphasis on the deadweight costs of taxes and subsidies and the fact that such costs generally rise at an increasing rate as taxes and subsidies increase. He suggests that an increase in the deadweight cost of a subsidy discourages pressure by the subsidized group while an increase in the deadweight cost of a tax encourages pressure by taxpayers. Consequently, deadweight costs give taxpayers an intrinsic advantage in the competition for influence. Groups that receive large subsidies presumably manage to offset their intrinsic disadvantage by efficiency, optimal size or easy access to political influence.

In Becker's analysis, all groups favour and lobby for efficient taxes, whereas efficient methods of subsidization raise subsidies and benefit recipients, but harm taxpayers unless recipients are induced to produce less pressure by a sufficiently rapid increase in their deadweight costs as their subsidy increases. He claims relevance for his theory not only to taxes and subsidies that redistribute income, but also to regulations and quotas, as well as to policies that raise efficiency by the production of public goods and the curtailment of other market failures. In his view, policies that raise efficiency are likely to win out in the competition for influence because they produce gains rather than deadweight costs, so that groups benefited have an intrinsic advantage compared to groups harmed. In Becker's world, where there is open competition between interest groups, together with free entry and exit, inefficient transfer mechanisms will not be widespread in political market equilibrium.

For a number of reasons, I do not share Becker's optimism regarding the impact of interest groups in democratic politics, at least in the absence of important constitutional constraints. Let me start with the free-rider problem emphasized by Mancur Olson in his seminal discussion of the logic of collective action (Olson 1965). The free-rider proposition asserts that in a wide range of situations, individuals will fail to participate in collectively profitable activities in the absence of coercion or of individually appropriable inducements (Stigler 1974). This proposition is easily illustrated.

Let the gain to an individual be equal to G if a collective activity is undertaken. For instance, G may be the individual's gain from a tariff which might be obtained by an effective interest group lobby. The cost of the collective action is C, and there are n identical self-seeking individuals. By hypothesis, the joint action is collectively profitable, so $nG > C$. However, the individual will refrain from joining the collective action if n is of some appreciable size, given his judgement that the viability of the action does not depend on his participation. If enough individuals free ride in this manner, the collective action will not be taken. Even though rides, like lunches, are never completely free, if *n* is large the free-rider problem is widely believed to be endemic.

Mancur Olson (1965) set out to prove logically that free-riding was not a universal problem for collective action but rather that it struck differentially at particular types of interest group, thereby providing unequal or asymmetric access to the political process. The paradox that he presented is that (in the absence of special arrangements or circumstances) large groups, at least if they are composed of rational individuals, will *not* act in their group interest. The reason for this is to be found in the publicness characteristics of the benefits that flow from successful collective action (Olson 1965, 1982). In such circumstances, interest groups will not exist unless individuals support them for some reason *other* than for the collective goods that they may provide.

In the case of government, of certain professional associations and of labour unions that have secured the political privilege of the closed shop, free-riding is overcome by the coercive powers that can be deployed against recalcitrant individuals. These coercive powers are usefully subsumed under the more general concept of *selective incentive* which explains almost all successful collective action in the case of large groups of individuals. A selective incentive is one that applies selectively to individuals depending on whether or not they contribute to the provision of the collective good.

A selective incentive may be positive or negative. Tax payments, for example, are obtained with the help of negative selective incentives, since those who are found not to have paid their taxes must suffer taxes, accumulated interest and additional penalties. Most of the dues extracted by strong trade unions are obtained through union shop, closed shop or agency shop arrangements which make dues paying more or less compulsory. Positive selective incentives are also commonplace. For example, many of the members of American farm lobbies have their dues deducted automatically from the 'patronage dividends' of farm co-operatives or included in the insurance premia paid to mutual insurance companies associated with the farm lobbies (Olson 1982). Any number of organizations with urban clients provide selective incentives in the form of insurance policies, publications, group air fares and other private goods made available at special discounts only to members.

Stigler (1974) has questioned Olson's by-product theory of selective incentives by challenging the assertion that an interest group would be able to charge more than the cost of the services supplied in the case of services that are appropriable as private goods. Surely, if an interest group seeks to add a charge for the provision of collective action, a rival supplier of those services, that undertakes no collective action, can undersell it. Even if those services, such as the collection of information, possess great economies of scale – are indeed natural monopolies – the argument is not affected: a rival group in a contestable market can still bid away the members of the interest group with a lower price.

There is evidence in support of Stigler's challenge. A particularly striking example is the experience of the American Automobile Association (AAA) which provides a number of selective incentives to attract funding for its lobbying activities. One such service is the provision of carefully designed route maps for members who request such assistance. The larger gasoline companies determined that they could provide route maps at a lower average price than the AAA because they diverted no part of the revenues for collective action. Thus, AAA suffered a considerable financial reverse and loss of membership. It is now much less active in political lobbying and focuses its activities much more specifically on its members' direct car needs.

Olson (1982), perhaps in response to Stigler-type criticisms, suggests that there is often a symbiotic relationship between the political power of a lobbying organization and the business institutions associated with it. This relationship often yields tax or other advantages for the business institutions. Moreover, the publicity and other information flowing out of the political arm of a movement often generates patterns of preference or trust that make business activities of the movement more remunerative. If so, the surpluses obtained indeed would provide positive selective incentives that recruit participants for the lobbying efforts. Olson offers no examples of such symbiosis. Evidently, the difference of opinion between Stigler and Olson concerns a matter of fact and must be resolved by sound empirical and institutional analysis.

Small groups, or occasionally large federal groups that are made up of many small groups, have an additional source of both negative and positive selective incentives. Most individuals value the companionship and respect of those with whom they socially interact. The censure or even the ostracism of those who fail to bear a share of the burdens of collective action sometimes can be an important selective incentive. Olson (1982) cites the example of British trade unionists who refuse to speak to unco-operative colleagues, that is, 'send them to Coventry'. Equally, members of an interest group may offer special honours to those who distinguish themselves by their lobbying efforts, thus providing positive selective incentives for such sacrifices.

As Olson recognizes, the availability of social selective benefits is limited by the social heterogeneity of some interest groups that could benefit from effective collective action. Even in the case of small groups, such social heterogeneity may prohibit the kinds of social interaction needed for social selective incentives to become meaningful. Many individuals resist extensive social interactions with those that they deem to have higher or lower intellectual or social status or greatly different tastes. Even non-conformist groups typically are composed of individuals who are more similar to each other than they are to the rest of society.

Moreover, socially-heterogeneous groups, even when they can be brought together at all, often will not agree on the exact nature of whatever collective good is at issue or on how much of it is worth buying. If collective action occurs under such circumstances, it does so at extra cost, especially for the leaders of whatever organization is involved. The American Bar Association (ABA) is an interesting example of this phenomenon. It holds most of its membership by the act of lobbying for licensing entry restrictions and cartel arrangements for the legal profession. Yet, its pursuit of other political agendas, notably the filling of federal judgeships with left-leaning judges and its endorsement of the pro-choice abortion stance, costs its leaders support among conservative and catholic attorneys, even extending to membership losses. Such behaviour ultimately could provoke a membership revolt and the removal of the politicized oligarchy that controls the ABA (Rowley 1992a). Alternatively, the ABA might segment into separate components, each reflective of its membership's collective action preferences.

If large interest groups must resort to selective incentives in order to pursue political lobbying, the environment is more promising for small interest groups, especially if they are composed of socially-homogeneous members. In small groups, individuals can avoid the free-riding prisoners' dilemma by behaving strategically, that is in ways that take account of the effect of their own choices on the behaviour of others. Although group-optimal outcomes may not be achievable, small interest groups often are able to engage in collective action without selective benefits. Olson refers to such groups as privileged groups. Privileged groups predictably will be disproportionately successful in political markets and will shift political outcomes away from median voters in favour of decisive minorities characterized by high preferences for specific policies.

Olson's logic of collective action, which I essentially endorse, is sharply different from that of Gary Becker. It focuses attention on the problem of asymmetric access to political markets, whereas Becker tends to emphasize equal access. It emphasizes problems of free-riding whereas Becker emphasizes deadweight social losses as the principal reason for collective action failures. It stresses, much more than Becker, the importance of small size as a determinant of lobbying impact. It highlights the cost of organizing interest groups and the difficulty of holding them together, whereas Becker tends to emphasize the ease of organization and the attraction of the gross returns to collective action (Crew and Rowley 1988a). In my view, the preponderance of the evidence is in favour of Olson, though further testing of both theories is desirable (see Mitchell and Munger 1991 for an excellent survey).

Let me now return to the relevance of my own rent-seeking insight to this debate over the role of interest groups. Writing in 1965, Olson could not be aware of the concept, and indeed he developed a theory of interest group behaviour that did not focus attention on the potentially high resource losses associated with lobbying competition. In 1982, however, although he did not discuss rent seeking as such, Olson clearly recognized the resource destruction implicit in bargaining over wealth transfers (Olson 1982, p. 43). He also recognized that the imposition of such public bads might be rational policy for small, well-organized interest groups. In his 1982 book, Olson endeavours to show that the social losses associated with government regulations can sometimes be colossal and that they are often the direct result of special interest lobbying. I thoroughly agree with this assessment.

In contrast, Becker (1983, 1985) more or less explicitly plays down the cost of rent seeking in his theory of pressure group competition. His 1983 article incorporates the normal costs of organization into the theory of pressure group organization. Except for this, however, the paper centres attention exclusively on Harberger triangles as a source of social loss and ignores Tullock rectangles. His 1985 paper notes that aggregate efficiency 'should be defined not only net of dead weight costs and benefits of taxes and subsidies, but also net of expenditures on the production of political pressure ... since these expenditures are only rent-seeking inputs into the determination of policies'. Becker does not follow through on this insight, but lamely concludes that 'little is known about the success of different kinds of political systems in reducing the waste from competition among pressure groups' (Becker 1985, p. 335).

Neither Olson nor Becker recognize that a principal determinant of the volume of resources dedicated to rent seeking is the magnitude of the rents available from the political market. This lacuna is especially important for Becker since such an interaction would significantly affect the nature of the Cournot-Nash equilibria that his model generates. I shall return to this issue of efficient rent-seeking in a later chapter (see Rowley, Shughart and Tollison 1987 for an empirical analysis of this issue).

In a way, it is fortunate that rent seeking is subject to the free-rider problem, since this undoubtedly reduces the total amount of rent-seeking activity and mitigates the resource cost to society. Unfortunately, Olson's logic of collective action impacts much more sharply upon the large numbers of heterogeneous individuals who wish to protect their property rights from the scavenging of rent-seekers, but who cannot organize effectively because of the free-rider problem. Rent-seekers typically exert disproportionate political influence because, if large, they can coerce their members or by-product their collective actions by the provision of selective incentives. If they are small and socially cohesive, they overcome the free-rider problem by strategic bargaining. In this perspective, interest group competition over transfers, contrary to Becker's theory, tends to be high cost both in terms of Harberger triangles and Tullock rectangles and constitutes a major ongoing threat to economic freedom.

I shall suggest, in the concluding chapter of this book, that constitutional constraints and institutional reforms can mitigate the extent of rent seeking on the part of interest groups (Buchanan 1980a and b). However, as Wagner (1987, 1988) has argued, the parchment of the Constitution itself is vulnerable to the guns of the special interests unless the Constitution itself can be protected by those general interests that find it so difficult to engage in democratic politics.

The Bureaucrats

Olson has been criticized (Mitchell and Munger 1991) for treating interest group lobbying as a pure demand phenomenon and for leaving out a powerful role for government. In my view, this criticism is misplaced since interest groups are located on both the demand and the supply sides of the political market and government serves primarily as a broker of the pressures that they can bring to bear. I am not convinced by North's (1990) suggestion that the state should be accorded a pre-eminent role in the formation and administration of property rules and rights, just as I am not convinced that it should be modelled as a revenue-maximizing Leviathan (Brennan and Buchanan 1980). Ultimately, empirical testing will determine which of the two models is correct, or whether indeed some other model is superior.

Nevertheless, I strongly endorse the view advanced by Niskanen (1971, 1975), building on earlier work by myself (Tullock 1965b) and by Downs (1967), that bureaucrats play a significant role in political markets not just as implementers of brokered policies but also on the demand side of the market. As such, they make a significant contribution to rent seeking and to the dissipation of wealth in society, taking full advantage of their status as small, privileged, homogeneous special interest groups empowered by their ability to coerce members and, thus, to overcome the free-rider effect.

In most democracies, including the United States, the bureaucracy carries a considerable political clout simply because its members make up a sizeable minority of the electorate. In the United States, government bureaucrats, federal, state and local combined, make up some 20 per cent of the total electorate, with a direct interest in expanding the scope of government. Even if their vote strength alone is recognized, as well-informed voters on issues central to their bureaux they would present a serious threat to the cause of limited government. For this reason, a case can be made for disenfranchising all government bureaucrats with respect to elections at their respective levels of the federal system. Of course, such a recommendation is not likely to survive log-rolling pressures in any pluralistic vote mechanism.

In any event, despite attempts by the Hatch Act in the United States to prohibit the use by bureaucrats of taxpayer monies to lobby the legislature, the bureaucrats exert an influence on the legislature significantly in excess of their vote power alone, in order to secure special interest benefits. Such benefits take the form of tenured employment, privileged health-care packages, contribution-free inflation-proof pension arrangements and the like, well beyond the expectations of private-sector employees. They also take the form of income and employment augmenting special interest legislation initiated by senior bureaucrats working within the so-called 'iron-triangles' composed of private interest groups, congressional committees and civil servants that log-roll among themselves to secure self-serving legislation financed by rationally ignorant and rationally casually ignorant voters. Such behaviour extends well beyond the federal bureaucracy and is evident, for example, in the success of the United States Post Office in protecting the letter mail from private competition and in securing for itself an overmanned and over-paid work-force financed by excessively high prices and public subsidies.

Let me focus on the rent-seeking potential of the federal bureaucracy through the formal lens provided by Niskanen (1971), where bureaux are defined as non-profit organizations financed, at least in part, by a periodic appropriation or grant, and where the rational behaviour of senior bureaucrats, responsible for the budgets and outputs of their bureaux, is subjected to careful institutional analysis. Niskanen's model, basic though it now may seem, provides a useful foundation for assessing the rent-seeking capabilities of government bureaux.

Niskanen uses the term *bureaucrat* to define the senior official of any bureau with a separate identifiable budget. These bureaucrats may be either career officials or individuals appointed directly by the elected executive. In his view, each bureaucrat seeks to maximize a utility function made up of the following variables: perquisites of the office, public reputation, power, patronage, output of the bureau, ease of making changes and ease of managing the bureau. All of these variables save the last two, in his view, are a positive monotonic function of the total budget of the bureau. Although the problems of making changes and the personal burdens of managing a bureau are often higher at higher budget levels, both tend to be reduced by increases in the total budget. Niskanen concludes, therefore, that budget maximization should be an adequate proxy even for bureaucrats with a relatively low pecuniary motivation and a relatively high

motivation for making changes in the 'public interest'. Evidence
strongly supports the hypothesis that most distinguished civil
servants substantially increase the budgets of the bureaux for
which they are responsible.

Given that bureaucrats seek to maximize the size of their
budgets, the constraint that ultimately limits the size of bureaux
is the requirement that a bureau, on the average, must supply
that output expected by the sponsor on its approval of the bureau's budget. The necessary condition for achieving the expected output is that the budget must be equal to or greater than
the minimum total expected costs of supplying this level of

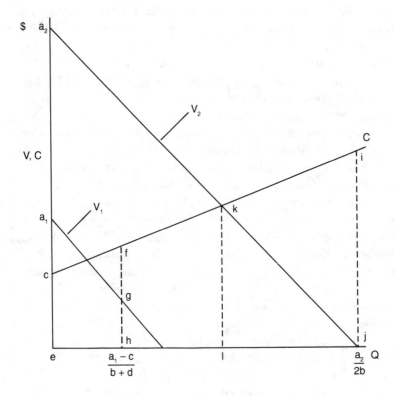

Figure 6.1   Budget-constrained and demand-constrained bureaux

output. This constraint is a critical element from which Niskanen develops a theory of supply by bureaux as outlined in Figure 6.1.

In Figure 6.1, a one-period relationship is outlined between a bureau, considered to be a monopoly supplier of the service, but a competitive purchaser of factor inputs and a legislative committee sponsor that is assumed not to exercise its potential monopoly power as a single buyer of the service, either because of lack of incentive or lack of opportunity. The total potential budget available to the bureau is represented by the budget-output function:

$$B = aQ - bQ^2, \quad 0 < Q < \frac{a}{2b}. \tag{6.3}$$

The minimal total cost is represented by the cost-output function:

$$TC = cQ + dQ^2, \quad 0 \le Q. \tag{6.4}$$

The budget constraint is represented as:

$$B \ge TC. \tag{6.5}$$

In Figure 6.1, V_1 represents lower demand conditions for the bureau's services, given by the marginal valuation function of the sponsoring legislative committee. The marginal cost function of the bureau is given by cC. The equilibrium output of the bureau, in this case, is *budget-constrained* at output $a_1 - c/b + d$, where the area of the polygon ea_1gh is equal to the area of the polygon ecfh. At this output, the bureau must be X-efficient since its total budget just equals its minimum total costs. The output of the bureau, however, is higher than optimum, assuming that the legislative committee's marginal valuation function somehow reflects aggregated voter's preferences. This is evidenced by the fact that marginal cost, hf, exceeds marginal value, hg, at equilibrium output.

For higher demand conditions represented by the marginal valuation function V_2, however, the equilibrium output of the bureau is *demand-constrained*, with the marginal value of output equal to zero. The total budget, given by the area of the triangle ea$_2$j, exceeds minimum total costs given by the polygon ecij. At the equilibrium output, the bureau is X-inefficient. Output is also higher than the 'optimal' level, with marginal cost at ji and with the marginal value of the service equal to zero.

Niskanen assumes that the bureau typically operates like a price discriminating monopolist securing for itself the maximum available surplus by offering a total output in return for a total budget appropriation. Bureaux are also assumed to benefit from better information regarding production costs than that available to congressional committees, thus protecting themselves from X-inefficiency challenges in the high-demand situation. There is a great deal of evidence that X-inefficiency permeates the federal bureaucracy, manifesting itself in overmanning, excessive on-the-job leisure, gold-plating of offices and cost ineffective input purchases, despite periodic investigations that draw the attention of casually-informed voters to the horror stories that not infrequently emerge.

Bureaux are adept at responding to threatened budget cuts with promises to eliminate services most valued by voters, thus marshalling the vote motive in favour of their bloated budgets. Politicians often lend credence to such defences, responding to special interests that rent-seek for the bureaucratic services that are under review. This interaction between bureaucrats, politicians and interest groups is referred to as the *iron triangle* by *cognoscenti* of Washington politics.

Two frequently-cited examples demonstrate the nature of this dangerous rent-seeking relationship. The first concerns the unjustifiable farm subsidy programme that I have already referred to in this book. Bureaucrats in the Department of Agriculture work closely with the farmers' lobbies and with congressmen on the agriculture committees of the US Congress to maintain inefficient farms, to grow and then to destroy uneconomic crops and to provide already affluent farmers with per-capita income subsidies several times higher than the annual earnings of the average US worker. Their own return is to be found in bureau budgets significantly higher than would be attainable if the US farming industry was to be returned to capitalist enterprise.

The second example concerns the military. The major armament manufacturers together with individuals who live around and service military installations ally themselves with congressmen dependent on defence industry contracts for their constituents and with bureaucrats from the Department of Defense whose budgets are dependent on high military appropriations from the US Congress. Such iron triangles are very resistant to voter attacks even in circumstances that clearly call for budgetary retrenchment.

The iron triangle hypothesis runs counter to recent theories advanced by Weingast and Moran (1983) and by Rowley and Elgin (1985) that suggest that the legislature itself monitors the behaviour of federal bureaux and periodically forces such bureaux to constrain their budget maximization objectives. If the congressional committees are controlled by high-demand congressmen, highly responsive to interest group pressures, they are highly unlikely to rein in the services of bureaux that feed those same interests. I am aware that some of the empirical evidence suggests that federal bureaux do adjust behaviour in response to changes in the composition of oversight and appropriations committees.

All such adjustments, however, are at the margin, and often are reflective of changes in the preferences or relative strengths of the interest groups that determine the political equilibrium. More sophisticated testing is necessary to determine whether Congress ever moves directly against the interest groups to weaken the base of the iron triangles and to lower bureau budgets in some public interested spirit. I doubt that much evidence of this sort will be uncovered, or that congressmen given to such flights of public interest would survive in politics.

One modification of Niskanen's theory that does merit attention is the notion advanced by Migué and Bélanger (1974) that bureaucrats may place less value on maximizing the size of their budgets than in maximizing the size of their *discretionary* budgets. If this is correct, then bureaucrats would select output i in Figure 6.1 where marginal cost equals marginal value, thus choosing to operate at the 'optimal' rate of output. Of course, the discretionary budget typically would be utilized to indulge the private preferences of bureaucrats, providing opportunities for luxurious office accommodation, for conferences and training sessions in exotic locations, for expensive business travel, support facilities and the like. As I have demonstrated in my own writings on income redistribution (Tullock 1983) such bureaucratic budget diversions are important reasons why poverty programmes fail to redistribute income to the poor.

A second modification (Peacock 1983) is the notion that bureaucrats may be lazy and evidence a high preference for work-avoiding activities. In the limit, they may prove to be so lazy that they do not actually produce any real output at all, hiding their ineptitude by bureaucratic obfuscation in areas where interest groups do not counter rational voter ignorance. An excellent example of such a bureau was the American Spruce Woods Corporation.

During World War I, airplanes were made of wood and the American Spruce Woods Corporation, with a director, four clerks and a chauffeur was set up in 1918 to expedite the movement of wood into the aircraft industry. Thereafter, the bureau did nothing. After World War II, Congress required that the Bureau of the Budget list all government corporations in its budget presentation. A vigilant congressman then queried the role of the Corporation and it was quietly disbanded. By that time, 28 years had elapsed and its six long-term employees had all qualified for federal government pensions.

In conclusion, bureaucrats themselves actively rent-seek through the political process, often conspiring with powerful interest groups and relevant congressional committees. In some cases, this rent seeking results in excessive rates of output, in others in bloated budgets and in yet others in manifest laziness and ineptitude. It should be kept in mind, however, that bureaucrats are often manipulated by other rent seekers, and that they certainly could not rent-seek as effectively as they do without the widespread compliance of politicians and the rational ignorance of much of the electorate.

The President and the Courts

The United States Constitution was devised to create a federal government whose powers would be checked by the separation of powers with no one of the three branches – legislative, executive or judicial – deemed to be superior to any of the others. In various ways, each branch technically has influence over each other branch and can use this influence to retaliate against unwarranted interference. In practice, as the Founding Fathers predicted, the legislature has proved to be the dominant branch able to secure the deference of the Supreme Court on most matters and able to dominate the President over budgetary policy in the absence of a line item veto. For this reason, my rent-seeking analysis largely focuses on the legislative market-place. Of course, this focus is even more justified in the case of parliamentary democracies such as the United Kingdom where the legislature is constitutionally supreme.

In the case of the United States, however, the potential influence of the courts and the President over the rent-seeking market should not be ignored as completely as it often is in the public choice literature. Let me briefly deal with each in turn, starting with the Supreme Court, which, in principle, is supposed to be an ultimate custodian of the Constitution, protected from political interference by the lifetime tenure and security of nominal income enjoyed by the justices.

In one view, advanced by Landes and Posner (1975), the independent judiciary plays an active role in promoting rent-seeking in the legislature by promoting durable legislation. Indeed, the judiciary helps current legislators to raise the rents available to successful interest groups by ensuring that the work of one legislature is not overturned by the next legislature. Landes and Posner (1975) argue that the courts tend to resolve legal disputes by reference to the actual intent of the propounding legislature. By so doing, their own budgets and the salaries of their judges and of their staffs tend to rise more rapidly than would be the case if they adopted a less accommodating stance. In my view, this theory of the independent judiciary ignores important political pressures that are applicable to the market for judgeships. Moreover, the econometric results obtained by Landes and Posner scarcely support their hypothesis. However, there may be something in the basic argument.

An alternative view (Rowley 1992b) sees the Supreme Court justices as pursuing their own individual agendas that made them attractive to the Presidents who appointed them at the time of their appointment. Where the Senate majority and the President are of the same political party at the time of appointment, this prediction seems to be particularly persuasive. Where they are not, ideological preferences predictably will be more muted and less unambiguous. Only if a sequence of like-minded presidents is able to appoint a majority of like-thinking justices (notably Reagan and Bush in recent years) is anything resembling a cohesive Supreme Court agenda likely to emerge. Rowley (1992b) has traced the reversal of Supreme Court judgments on takings cases since 1986 which, if sustained, will slow the pace of development of rent-seeking through the US legislature. Evidently, such an agenda could fade in an unfavourable political climate or in the wake of new appointments to the High Court following the election of a left-leaning democrat to the Presidency. Of course, if a left-leaning majority dominates the Supreme Court (the Warren Court) and defers to a democratic majority legislature, then the Landes and Posner (1975) hypothesis becomes extremely plausible.

The impact of the President on the rent-seeking equilibrium brokered by the legislature is similarly ambiguous. Following the idea of Landes and Posner (1975), Crain and Tollison (1979) hypothesized that the veto powers exercisable by a President, designed to force the legislature into supra-majority voting on new legislation, itself extended the perceived durability of existing legislation. In this view, the legislature and the President are seen as *de facto* colluders, purveying long-term legislation to the

dominant interest groups. Econometric results offer some support for their hypothesis. Once again, this theory seems to me to
over-generalize. Surely much depends on whether the President
and the legislature share the same political perspective and, if
not, the particular time-sequence in which new legislation is
presented to the President for his signature.

In the alternative view (Rowley 1992a), which may be especially relevant when the President's party does not control the
legislature, the President may intervene to destabilize the existing political equilibrium, either by log-rolling or by direct challenges to the legislative process. Furthermore, the President may
appoint bureaucrats whose specific purpose is to make use of
available bureaucratic discretion to effect policies that are not
fully endorsed by the legislative majority. The outcomes of such
intervention for rent-seeking equilibria are not unambiguous. If
my judgement is correct that the electoral college constituency
is less dominated by special interests than the constituencies of
senatorial congressmen, then presidential interventions, where
effective, will typically mitigate rent-seeking, most especially
during the first term of any given president's incumbency.

For the most part, I am inclined to focus attention on the
legislature, where the rent-seeking process is basically centred,
and to view the courts and the President as side-players, who,
occasionally, become more important.

7.   Efficient Rent-Seeking

If a given rent is available from the legislature, how much rent seeking will this given rent attract? This question is extremely important given my insight that a great deal of rent-seeking behaviour may be wasteful of scarce resources. It is instructive to answer this question within the framework of specific rent-seeking games, given that most rents are competed for, often in circumstances where the highest bidder receives at least a large part of the available rent (Peltzman 1976).

An early illustration of a rent-seeking game in which the total amount of the rent-seeking outlay exactly equals the available rent (the exact dissipation outcome) was provided by Posner (1975) in his widely-cited paper on the social costs of monopoly and regulation. Posner posited a situation in which ten firms vie for a government monopoly which carries with it a present value rent of one million dollars. He asserts that each firm has an equal probability (.1) of obtaining the rent, that each firm is risk neutral and that constant costs hold universally. In such circumstances, each firm will spend resources on rent seeking equal to one hundred thousand dollars, the expected present value of the prize, in an attempt to obtain the monopoly. Only one firm will succeed and its costs will be much smaller than the monopoly profits; but the total costs of obtaining the monopoly – counting losers' expenditures as well as winners' – will be the same as under certainty. Most of the costs in fact are made in unsuccessful attempts to seek rents – and not surprisingly these may be overlooked in empirical studies of the cost of rent seeking to society.

Posner's exact dissipation hypothesis is popular among the small group of scholars who attempt to calculate rent-seeking costs (including Posner himself) no doubt because it facilitates empirical work. If the entire Tullock rectangle is to be wasted, this is an area which can be reasonably approximated, given basic information on costs and demand elasticities and then be measured, if necessary, nationwide. Moreover, even if Posner's theory is generalized, to take account of free entry into the bidding mechanism, the underlying exact dissipation holds in the equilibrium solution. Although the winner receives ever more of the available rent as a super-normal return on its own rent-seeking investment, the equilibrium will not provoke subsequent rent seeking by others as long as durability was fundamental to the initial rent-seeking game. (But see Crew and Rowley 1988b when durability is not anticipated.)

Somewhat ironically, the exact dissipation outcome, which is not at all attractive from the perspective of Paretian welfare economics, has become known in the literature as the *efficient rent-seeking* outcome following my 1980 article on that topic (Tullock 1980) which questioned the likelihood of such an outcome in the real world. In that paper I outlined a range of rent-seeking models, in which the competitive process leads either to under- or to over-dissipation of the available rents, and in which rent seeking does not take place under the constant cost conditions specified by Posner (1975). This paper has generated a considerable volume of articles, none of which has succeeded in resolving the problem that I posed, although in many ways the important parameters have now been identified (see Rowley, Tollison and Tullock 1988). Issues such as risk aversion, arbitrary limits on the number of bidders, imperfect information, and decreasing and increasing returns turn out to be very important (Corcoran 1984, Corcoran and Karels 1985, Higgins, Shughart and Tollison 1985, Hillman and Katz 1984, Rogerson 1982, Tullock 1980, 1985, 1987a, 1988b, 1989).

Although I can easily generate over-dissipation outcomes, it might seem that this solution is unlikely to hold, at least in respect to games where competitors become aware that they are engaged in a game *ex ante* which lowers their expected net wealth. If over-dissipation occurs, and the rent-seeking outlays are wasted, a society which tolerates the creation of rents by government may end up impoverished. In the extreme case depicted by Magee, Brock and Young (1989), for example, 100 per cent of the economy may end up devoted to lobbying. As I note in my 1989 book, the rent-seeking industry appears to be too small, at least in the United States, to give credibility to the over-dissipation hypothesis (Tullock 1988a).

Under-dissipation where rent-seekers, as a whole, outlay less than the total value of the rent available is a much more likely outcome. Hillman and Katz (1984) have demonstrated that risk aversion among the rent-seekers will generate such an outcome. Rogerson (1982) has shown that comparative advantage among monopolizing inputs also causes under-dissipation. I have shown that game-specific factors plausibly will produce such an outcome (Tullock 1980, 1985). In my view, increasing and decreasing returns to scale are potentially very important factors.

Suppose that diseconomies of scale dominate the rent-seeking game. Under such circumstances, the smaller the enterprise, the more profitable it is, and even with free entry and perfect competition, super-normal returns persist. In the limit, an infinite number of disappearingly small enterprises would outlay only a small proportion of the total rents provided by the competition. In reality, there are practical limits to such a process. A large number of individuals can write letters to their congressmen; but each must attach a 29 cent stamp to his letter. This lower bound will limit the number of competitors, although evidence of abnormally high returns may stimulate additional socially wasteful outlays.

Suppose instead that there are economies of scale. Over-dissipation is then highly likely unless one rent-seeker makes a preclusive bid to keep other rent-seekers out before the active competition commences. There are dangers that such bids will be ill thought-out because they must be made in haste and will turn out to be misguided. For example, Sony recently outlayed $1^{1}/_{2}$ million dollars to buy a movie script and added to this an outlay of 45 million dollars to make the movie. On completion, they showed the movie to trial audiences and realized that it was so poor that it could not be released. Explaining this error, a senior executive of a rival company remarked that 'this business is so unscrupulous and so cut-throat that there is no time to think about anything'. This is very much the environment in which preclusive bid calculations must be effected. Any social pay-offs to available scale economies may well be squandered in a sequence of risky gambles.

The most desirable rent-seeking outcome is that in which rent-seeking costs are zero and in which rent seeking results in wealth transfers rather than in the dissipation of wealth. The Chicago School (Becker 1983, 1985) tends to promulgate transfer models with such characteristics, emphasizing the endogeneity of transfers and the incentives for interest groups to avoid dissipation. There is no evident competitive mechanism that ensures such socially-desirable outcomes. If scarce resources are dedicated to rent seeking, clearly they cannot be used elsewhere to create producers' and/or consumers' surplus over cost. In my view, the zero dissipation result is a figment of neoclassical theorists' imaginations. Such evidence as is available offers no support for any such hypothesis, at least in economies like the United States where expensive election campaigns typically waste whatever initial transfers individual congressmen manage to accrue.

8. The Transitional Gains Trap

One of the major activities of modern government is the granting of special privileges to various groups of politically-influential people. On the whole, the profit record of such protected organizations does not seem to differ systematically from that of the unprotected sections of the economy. This simple observation led me to raise questions that culminated in my theory of the *transitional gains trap* (Tullock 1975). My thesis is that there are only transitional gains to be made when the government establishes privileges for a group of people. The successors to the original beneficiaries will not normally make exceptional profits. Unfortunately, they will usually be injured by any cancellation of the original gift. It would seem, as David Friedman has put it, that 'the government cannot even give anything away'.

Let us consider a very simple example of government monopoly creation, namely the taxi medallion system basically as it operates in New York City. In the absence of entry restrictions, the taxicab market is extremely competitive with price equal to marginal cost and with only normal returns available to taxicab operators. By artificially restricting supply, the freely-distributed medallions raise price above marginal cost, transferring some consumers' surplus to the taxicab owners and imposing a deadweight social loss on some would-be consumers who now find themselves displaced from the market. Ignoring any rent-seeking costs that initially induce the government to monopolize the taxicab industry, taxicab owners fortunate enough to obtain medallions clearly gain a great deal.

Now revisit the taxicab market after a number of years have elapsed. The capital value of the monopoly profit has been fully taken into account throughout the industry. New taxicab firms enter only by purchasing the requisite number of medallions on the open market. With the monopoly profit fully capitalized, they obtain only normal profits. The surviving original owners now have opportunity costs equivalent to the value of the medallions that they hold. On these costs, they also receive only normal returns. The customers remain worse off because the price remains higher than competitive cost.

The medallion holders will lobby vigorously against any attempt to withdraw the medallion scheme, many of them arguing with justice that they have paid out capital, investing in medallions as a prerequisite for entering the taxicab market. In a very real sense they have established property rights in a system that is the creation of the New York City government. The public choice pressures against deregulation in such circumstances predictably will be well nigh insurmountable, to say nothing of arguments based on property rights and even social justice.

The trap may be even tighter where government subsidies are concerned. Suppose that the government decides to pay manufacturers a subsidy on each chocolate bar sold. Initially, this enables the manufacturers of chocolate bars to make super-normal profits. These profits, in the long run, attract other companies into the industry, render the chocolate bar industry uneconomically large, and lower profits once again to the competitive norm. The economy as a whole is smaller and less efficient than in the pre-subsidy situation and no manufacturer is making any gains.

Now suppose that a proposal emerges to terminate the subsidy. The chocolate bar manufacturers predictably will fight hard to retain the arrangement, recognizing that its termination must impose sharp short-run losses on existing manufacturers until total capacity falls to that capable of supporting the sale of unsubsidized chocolate bars. In addition, the subsidies benefit specifically and perhaps significantly those individuals who purchase chocolate bars. If they can overcome the logic of collective action, such individuals will join the manufacturers in the pro-subsidy lobby. At least, the manufacturers can target the chocolate bar consumers and dispel their casual ignorance as they decide whether or not to vote, and for whom, in upcoming elections.

The problem posed by the transitional gains trap is the ratchet-like nature of rent seeking. Once a rent has been successfully sought out through government lobbying, it is very difficult to remove even after it has ceased to produce positive profits for its rent-seeking beneficiaries. Its elimination almost always implies losses for those who now exercise the privilege. To avoid such losses, they will rent-seek yet again to retain the privileges. Politicians are rightly reluctant to inflict direct losses on specific sections of the electorate – inevitably a vote-losing strategy.

The general interest, if it can overcome the logic of collective action, may occasionally convince the median voter that the rent-seekers in question are entirely undeserving of their rents and that economic well-being would increase if they were stripped of their privileges. It is even possible that the US deregulation process of the 1980s was facilitated by electing Ronald Reagan to the presidency on just such propaganda as this. Experience indicates, however, that it is much easier to attack the property rights of those who have succeeded in private competitive markets than it is to restore such rights to those who have had them seized. The rent-seekers, after all, are specialized in manipulating propaganda and public relations for self-seeking ends.

More realistically, government privileges may be vulnerable when they no longer serve the purpose for which they were originally designed. The New York taxicab medallion usefully illustrates this possibility. The number of taxicab medallions in New York has remained unchanged for a very long period of time. It is somewhat unlikely that the demand and cost conditions in the taxicab market have continuously been such that an unchanged number of cabs has maximized monopoly gains. It is more than likely that the monopolists are unable fully to exploit the consumer because the number of medallions is no longer optimal. The medallion holders may be reluctant to lobby to change the number of medallions for fear of provoking voter reaction. In such circumstances, a feeble push for deregulation may encounter little resistance.

The regulated sector is likely to fall behind generally, because the protection from competition reduces incentives to cut costs, to innovate and to pay close attention to changing consumer preferences. In such circumstances, the original rents slowly disappear, leaving the sector vulnerable to internal reform. The Soviet Empire, by 1989, was in just such a situation. Internal reforms are occurring there despite the 30 million card-carrying communist party 'medallion holders' whose livelihoods have been jeopardized by the bonfire of privileges.

In general, however, the transitional gains trap is a warning and not an opportunity. It is very costly to facilitate successful rent seeking because it is very difficult indeed to deregulate under conditions of democracy (Crew 1987).

9. Rent Protection, Rent Extraction and Rent Creation

Consideration of transitional gains leads naturally to the subject of rent protection – the problem of retaining rents once they have been secured from the political market. Not only do individuals deploy scarce resources to seek out rents, they also deploy scarce resources to protect their rents from other rent-seekers and from rent-avoiders. Rowley and Tollison (1986) set out the key issues that govern any rent-seeking, rent-protection game in their study of trade protection.

They assume, following Stigler (1971) and Peltzman (1976) that the market in regulation responds even-handedly to the precise balance of dollar-votes expended in the battle over an available privilege. They further assume, for the sake of argument, that the consumer interest is not entirely eroded by free-riding. In such circumstances, the durable privilege defined by the regulation market will not secure maximum available rents for a successful rent-seeker. Equilibrium will confirm output in excess of, and price less than, the full monopoly potential, reflecting the marginal impact of consumer outlays in the political market. Figure 9.1 illustrates such an outcome.

In Figure 9.1, producers rent-seek a full monopoly right, at price OA and output OQ_m. Consumers defend the competitive solution, at price OE and output OQ_c. All such expenditures represent social waste. The political market brokers an equilibrium at price at OF, somewhere between OA and OE, weighting equally the dollar votes of producers and consumers. In their example, the political price, OF is established slightly above the midpoint OA – OE, reflecting differentially heavy lobbying by the producers. Specifically, the producers outlay the present value

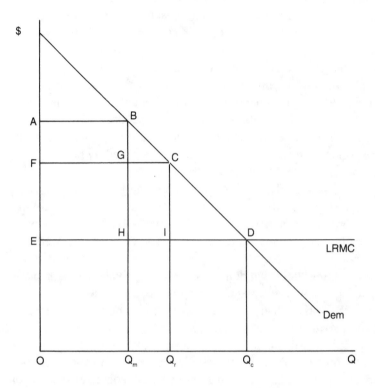

Figure 9.1   The Rowley–Tollison model of rent-seeking and rent protection

of the rectangle FCIE to lift price from OE to OF. Consumers outlay the present value of the trapezoid ABCF to hold price below the monopoly level OA. Since FCIE exceeds ABCF, the political price OF reflects the producers' lobbying advantage.

In Rowley's and Tollison's example, the social cost of the partial monopoly outcome, assuming that all outlays are dissipated as social waste, is identical to that of the full monopoly outcome in the absence of rent avoidance by consumers. The area ABCF + FCIE + CID is exactly equivalent to the area ABDE. This result is particular to the assumptions employed but

illustrates the general nature of rent-seeking, rent-protection battles under conditions of rational expectations. Once a particular
rent has been extracted, the threat of rent-protection outlays
predictably dampens reform initiatives, as the transitional gains
trap insight clearly implies. Viewed dispassionately, the fact that
rent protection outlays waste scarce resources dampens the
social welfare argument in favour of deregulation at least where
time rates of discount are high. Of course, social welfare arguments have little impact on political markets, which typically
respond to the redistributionist forces identified by public choice
theory (Crew and Rowley 1988b).

In 1987, McChesney advanced this analysis significantly by
integrating the role of the politician into the basic rent-seeking,
rent-protection model (see also McChesney 1991). McChesney
modelled politicians not as mere brokers redistributing wealth in
response to competing private demands, but as independent actors making their own demands to which private actors respond.
This conceptual reversal of roles, in turn, forces consideration of
the ways other than rent creation whereby politicians can gain
from private parties.

Political office confers a 'property right', not just to legislate
rents, but to impose costs. A politician can gain by forbearing
from exercising his right to impose burdensome restrictions on
private actions. For example, the passage of sharply focused
taxes and regulations will reduce the returns that private capital-
owners receive from their skills and investments. In order to
protect these returns, private owners have an incentive to strike
bargains with legislators, to pay extortion, as long as such extortion outlays are lower than the expected losses from compliance
with the threatened law. Such transfers create incentives for
private actors to invest in specific capital, since such investments render them especially vulnerable to the politicians' protection racket. Figure 9.2 illustrates McChesney's theory.

Figure 9.2 depicts an industry in which producers have differ-
ing amounts of entrepreneurial capacity or some firm-specific,
fixed-cost asset. The industry supply curve in the absence of
regulation (S_0) thus is upward sloping. Returns to entrepreneur-

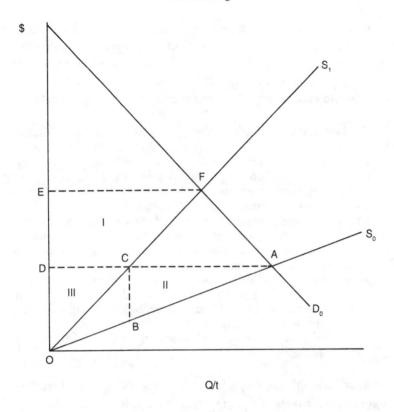

Figure 9.2 The McChesney model of rent extraction

ship and specific assets come as rents out of producers' surplus, OAD. Regulatory measures could be identified that would increase costs for all firms, but more for marginal firms, rotating the industry supply curve to S_1. To inframarginal producers, regulation is advantageous as long as there is a net increase in rents. In Figure 9.2, area I is greater than area II (CDEF > ABC); thus the gains from higher prices exceed the losses due to fewer sales.

However, rent creation by a government mandated shift from S_0 to S_1 is not the only option open to politicians. *Existing* private rents rewarding specific assets are greater than the rents that can be created by regulation (OAD > CDEF). Regulatory measures can be identified that would expropriate this producers' surplus. Once such regulation is threatened, the price that producers would pay politicians in return for governmental inaction would exceed any payment for rent-creating regulations:

> 'Milker bills' is one term used by politicians to describe legislative proposals intended only to squeeze private producers for payments not to pass the rent-extracting legislation. 'Early on in my association with the California legislature, I came across the concept of milker-bills – proposed legislation which had nothing to do with milk to drink and much to do with money, the mother's milk of politics' ... Representative Sam, in need of campaign contributions has a bill introduced which excites some constituency to urge Sam to work hard for its defeat (easily achieved), pouring funds into his campaign coffers and 'forever' endearing Sam to his constituency for his effectiveness. Milked victims describe the process simply as blackmail and extortion. The threats are made quite openly. One reads, for example, that 'House Republican leaders are sending a vaguely threatening message to business political action committees: Give us more, or we may do something rash.' (McChesney 1987, p. 108).

Rent extraction can succeed only to the extent that threats to expropriate private rents are credible. To this end, politicians may sometimes have to enact legislation extracting private rents from owners who do not pay up, just as the *Cosa Nostra* occasionally burns down the buildings of those who fail to pay its protection levies. Evidently, as McChesney concludes, there is no such thing as a free market, at least in countries like the United States that have abandoned all constitutional protection for economic rights and have allowed free rein to majoritarian politics.

10.   The Cost of Rent Seeking

The measurement of rent-seeking costs is a treacherous business even in Western economies that are relatively open and well-endowed with statistical sources. The concept itself is nebulous, even when rent seeking is restricted to government-targeted outlays, for all the reasons outlined in this book. Not surprisingly, empirical estimates of the social cost of rent seeking fluctuate widely from study to study both for the United States and elsewhere. I shall not attempt to survey the growing literature in detail, but rather will sample the results to indicate the lack of any general consensus on this issue.

The first attempt at measurement was that by Krueger (1974), whose crude estimates suggested that the value of rents in India in 1964 amounted to 7.3 per cent of India's national income and that rents from import licences alone in Turkey in 1968 approximated 15 per cent of Turkey's gross national product. Estimates of this order, even for Third World countries, certainly helped to put the rent-seeking problem on the economics map. Of course, questions remain as to what proportion of these rents was actually wasted and what proportion changed hands as undiluted transfers of wealth. The continuing impoverished state of both countries lends credibility to the social waste hypothesis.

In 1975, Posner used the concept of the Tullock rectangle to raise Harberger's calculation that the social cost of monopoly in the United States was a mere 0.1 per cent of gross national product to the much more significant figure of 3.4 per cent (but see Fisher 1985). He also noted that the regulated sector of the US economy, unjustifiably, had been omitted from Harberger's estimations. Since then, the studies have mounted rapidly and with them, generally, the estimated costs of rent-seeking behaviour. Ross (1984), for example, estimated that trade-related rent-

seeking in Kenya accounted for some 38 per cent of that country's gross domestic product.

Recently, work by Laband and Sophocleus (1988), Magee,
Brock and Young (1989) and Murphy, Schleifer and Vishny
(1990) have attempted to use attorneys as a proxy for rent-
seeking waste, and have suggested through regression analysis
that attorneys in the US reduce income by as much as 45 per
cent. Laband (forthcoming) in a more speculative study that
includes locks, insurance and police expenditures as proxies for
rent-seeking waste, estimates that some 50 per cent of United
States gross national product was wasted in rent seeking in 1985.
I am sceptical of these measures, given the almost metaphysical
nature of the rent-seeking concept itself at the present time.

In my book, *The Economics of Special Privileges and Rent
Seeking* (1989), I attempt to explain the apparently small size of
the rent-seeking industry, given the magnitude of the rents available through the political process. If one visits Washington DC,
or indeed any other national or state capital, one is immediately
impressed by the number of fancy restaurants and night-clubs
that are frequented by the lobbyists for private corporations and
other special interests to entertain high-ranking government officials.

However, the outlays on lobbying appear to be trivial in com-
parison with the government largesse that is handed out. Not all
of the difference can be made up in the form of bribes and illicit
campaign contributions, although these are far from trivial even
in the US where corruption may be less pronounced than in most
Third World countries. Although legitimate campaign contributions attract a great deal of publicity, these also amount to only a
small percentage of the value of the special privileges that are
routinely dispensed by government.

Let me conclude by emphasizing that we do not actually have
good measures of rent-seeking cost at the present time for reasons both theoretical and empirical. We do have sound theoretical reasons for believing that rent-seeking costs are relatively
high and for suspecting that many are hidden, taking the form of
failed bids, aborted enterprise, uncharted waste and threatened

but never activated public policies. We also know that most senior executives of large companies and trade associates now spend a fair amount of time in Washington. In 1890, they never went there at all.

11. Feasible Political Reform to Protect Property Rights

Vincent Ostrom (1984) has explained clearly that the use of government authority involves a difficult Faustian bargain. Government involves the use of an instrument of evil, force and compulsion in human affairs, because of the good that it is hoped will come out of that evil. We can hope that the good that comes from this evil instrument will be great, and equally we can hope that the evil that results will be small. What I have been discussing to this point is the evil that results because of government's ability to use force. The evil that has been done is, I fear, gigantic. In any event it is far removed from being small.

The relevant question, of course, is whether there is anything better. We need government to protect us from each other and to secure us from foreign threats. To be sure, those foreign threats might seem weaker these days. And doubtlessly they are at this time. But one of the great certainties of history is that things change. Francis Fukuyama (1992) argues that whatever changes the future may bring, the chaos and bloodshed of the past are unlikely to be part of it. He may be right. We will have to wait and see. I am not so confident that the end of history is at hand. More likely is the possibility that we are at some plateau or resting point, with further threats to come.

Even if we set aside external threats, the Faustian bargain still characterizes internal politics. The major justification for government is to secure our rights from violation from our fellows and to provide those public goods that cannot be well provided through ordinary market processes. The ability of government to use its monopoly of legitimate force is central to the fulfilment of these tasks. But monopoly is never used for good only. The temptation to commit evil will often prove irresistible. Rather than protecting rights from violation, government power will often be used as an instrument of violation, as much of the literature on rent seeking notes. And rather than providing genuine public goods, government will often use its authority and its taxing power to provide private goods desired by particular, politically-influential people at public expense.

The Faustian dilemma is intrinsic in the nature of government. We cannot hope to abolish it. All we can hope for is to be able to mitigate the evil consequences through reducing the frequency and vigour with which rent-seeking activities are pursued. But how can this be done? There is no simple, magic recipe to be followed. I can say this with assurance, having spent the bulk of my professional career thinking of such matters. All we can hope for is to secure modest improvements when the opportunity arises. I have no utopian plan to offer, only a few suggestions for modest improvement. But we must not forget that even the longest journey must begin with the first step (Rowley 1988b).

What I shall do in this closing chapter is review five modest steps towards political reform that would better protect property rights: qualified majority voting, greater use of referenda, required balanced budgets, limits on the size and extent of government, and better constitutional enforcement. In describing these steps as modest, I do not mean to imply that I think any of them is feasible politically. All I mean is that they are simple, easily understandable reforms that would improve matters. How much improvement is hard to say, but the change would be in the right direction in any case. Moreover, I am confident other people will have other good ideas that they can add, with the result that we might be able to come up with a list of quite substantial improvements after all (Rowley 1987).

In 'Some Problems of Majority Voting' (Tullock 1959), I described how simple majority voting led to a wasteful expansion in the size of government. Essentially this was because the members of winning majority coalitions were able to secure personal price reductions because of their ability to force part of the cost of their desired programmes on to others. This expansion in the size of government is a simple proposition of elementary demand theory. Someone who likes to go to movies will go to more movies if the price is cut in half. Majority voting essentially allows this to happen. The members of a winning coalition get price cuts to the extent that the taxes to finance the programmes are paid for by outsiders (Buchanan, Rowley and Tollison 1987).

To be sure, people who are in winning coalitions on one issue can be in losing coalitions on another issue. It might seem as though things would even out in the long run. But this is not so, even ignoring Keynes's point that we would be dead by then anyhow. Let me give you an example. Suppose meals are eaten and paid for in common. The population is roughly equally divided between those who prefer meat and those who prefer fish. Further, within each category there are cheap meals and expensive meals. Depending on their tastes, people would eat the kind of food they prefer, and in their preferred mix of cheap and expensive portions. Suppose the population consists of people who would eat cheaply five days a week.

Now suppose the supply of meals is to become a collective budgetary choice, and first the meat preferrers are on the winning side. Since roughly half of the cost is placed on to the fish preferrers, it is unlikely that the meat preferrers would choose expensive meals on only two days. How many expensive meals they would choose would depend on their demand for expensive meals in relation to the lower price that the winning coalition secures. Should the relationship be reversed and the fish preferrers be the winning coalition, they too will increase the frequency with which they eat expensive meals. Throughout the entire society the costliness of meals rises because of majority voting. Yet everyone is worse off; they are eating expensive meals five days a week, say, and paying for them, whereas they would prefer to eat expensive meals only two days a week.

Qualified majority voting mitigates these damages imposed by simple majority voting. The extreme case of qualified majority voting is unanimity, which was examined in *The Calculus of Consent* (Buchanan and Tullock 1962). But any increase in the voting rule above a simple majority increases the share of the cost that the members of a winning coalition must bear. A rule of three-quarters majority, for instance, would tend to mean that members of a winning coalition would bear three-quarters of the cost of their choices, and so would support lesser, inefficient increases in government than they would under simple majority voting.

Another voting change that would generally reduce rent seeking is to allow greater use of referenda. Switzerland, which permits referenda on an immense number of things, has the smallest government of any European nation. The Swiss government is also highly decentralized, with Cantonal and Communal activities being a major portion of a governmental activity. To be sure, the referendum does not eliminate rent seeking, but only restricts it. In the United States perhaps only California even remotely approaches the extensive Swiss usage, and California clearly has a great deal of rent seeking. But do not forget that California's pioneering effort at tax limitation was the outcome of a referendum.

Referenda work best to restrict rent seeking when they are restricted to a single issue. With such a restriction, a measure will pass only if it benefits a majority of voters. This still leaves plenty of scope for transfers from losing minorities to winning majorities, along with the inefficient expansion in government that this allows. But it does cut out the log-rolling packages where each component offers large benefits to intense minorities at general expense. A legislature can vote on a project to aid farmers, with the representatives of, say, the inner cities being promised something in another bill in exchange for their support. Such trades are difficult in referenda though, unfortunately, they are not impossible. In Tucson, where I live, we recently had a referendum on a large collection of street repair and school building projects that were arranged as a gigantic log-roll to secure sufficient support for the package, when no single item would be likely to pass.

Another simple change that would protect property rights would be to require the federal government to operate with a balanced budget. Many state governments already operate with such a requirement, and they get their business done. Just as surely, state governments are full of rent seeking, so a balanced budget requirement will not eliminate rent seeking. But it can reduce it. Without a balanced budget requirement, politicians can promise favours to constituents without having to impose taxes sufficient to pay for those favours. Deficit finance makes it possible to postpone part of the cost into the future. A balanced budget requirement would force politicians more fully to assess the opposition to higher taxation that would accompany proposals for increased spending (Buchanan 1958, Buchanan and Wagner 1977).

Direct limits on the size and growth of government would also be a simple device that would help to restrict rent seeking. I have already mentioned the tax limitation referendum in California. There is no reason that something similar could not be imposed on the central government. A government that was tax-limited to 20 per cent of national output would be a much smaller government than we now have, though I am confident a great deal of rent-seeking activity would still be going on. It has always struck me as a little curious that proposals for tax limitation typically seek to freeze the relative size of government where it currently is. This might seem to be a reasonable and expedient compromise with existing political interests, though I see no reason why some provision could not be allowed for relative shrinkages in government over time. Why must we always see governments asking for tax increases? Why not have political parties competing to offer tax reductions?

To this point, I have advanced some rather traditional proposals that are easily implementable and would restrict rent seeking, though would not eliminate it. Let me now offer some more speculative remarks. Surely, one way to reduce the amount of rent seeking dramatically would be to require members of Congress to read the bills that they pass. It would be nice to be able to get the members of Congress actually to think about those bills, but even getting them to read them would be a great improvement. We could also hope that when legislation provides for regulations being issued by, say, the Secretary of the Interior, that the Secretary of the Interior would also read those regulations.

A friend of mine in Connecticut once became part of a group that would read all proposed legislation before the Connecticut legislature, in order to advise a recently-elected legislator. The members of the group, however, soon stopped their reading. It was a lot of work, the material was as dull as it was prolix, and the representative paid little or no attention to the group because she was too busy making trades and deals with the other members of the legislature.

I know of no practical method of implementing such an idea, but merely to articulate it makes the point: there is far too much legislation, most of which is written by special-interest groups, and about which even the most conscientious members of a legislature could not keep informed.

Televising Congressional proceedings is, however, an activity about which something can be done. At the moment, Congressional rules prohibit the television camera from moving away from the speaker. As a result it is impossible for viewers to tell that the only members in the chamber are those designated by their parties to sit in at all times and see to it that nothing untoward happens. Usually, three of four of these watchmen are present, and sometimes a few more individuals are present. Suppose the television cameras were free regularly to scan the benches of the House and Senate, thus permitting people at home to witness the empty chambers. Such a change would doubtlessly lead to some revision in Congressional proceedings, or possibly even the elimination of television, save for limited, special occasions where good attendance can be assured. Yet this, too, would be a minor reform, because the bulk of the damage is done before a bill gets to the floor of Congress.

Finally, I should like to close by re-examining some ideas on 'Constitutional Mythology' that I published in 1965 (Tullock 1965a). We continually hear statements to the effect that the Supreme Court is the ultimate arbiter of what the Constitution means. This is pure myth. While myths can be entertaining and even illuminating so long as they are treated as literature, they can be dangerous if they are believed and acted upon. This is true for the myth that holds that the Constitution means what the Supreme Court says it means. Precisely what the Constitution sought to avoid by its system of checks and balances was a situation where one of the branches of government became dominant over the other two. Rather what the Constitution sought to create was a situation where all the branches of government were subservient to the Constitution. Constitutionality, in other words, would be tested by a concordance among the three branches of government, and most surely would *not* be tested by one branch dictating to the other two.

This understanding held sway until recent times. This meant that the Supreme Court would refuse to issue orders enforcing what it regarded as unconstitutional acts by Congress or the President. In like manner, the President would refuse to enforce what he regarded as unconstitutional rulings by Congress or the Supreme Court. For instance, President Andrew Jackson responded to a ruling of Chief Justice John Marshall in the *Cherokee Indian Cases* with the remark: 'John Marshall has made his decision, now let him enforce it' (Warren 1922). In other words, a proper understanding of our system of checks and balances, an understanding which has disappeared during the post-war period along with the eruption of rent seeking, would regard all three branches of government as independently charged to uphold the Constitution, and with no one branch being superior to the other two branches.

Such a system of concordant authority would be similar to the framework within the Western legal tradition developed until the past two centuries or so (Berman 1983). The Western legal tradition began in the 11th century, with the joint autonomy of ecclesiastical and secular authorities. To be sure, there were continual conflicts along the boundaries. But, for the most part, both authorities were autonomous and most people owed partial allegiance to both authorities. The sentiment commonly voiced that law transcends politics was a reflection of this situation, for both monarch and church were bound by law, as evidenced by the need for concordance between the two. Our Founders recognized that religious authority had lost its transcendent position in society, to be sure, but they also recognized that the existence of competing authorities for constitutionality were central to the maintenance of free institutions. For to the extent governance requires a concordance among independent sources of authority, that governance will tend to reflect the common or general interests of those being governed (Wagner 1987, 1988). That was the promise of the American Founding; it is a promise that we dearly need to relearn today.

References

Barzel, Y. and Silberberg, E. (1973), 'Is the Act of Voting Rational?', *Public Choice*, 16, 51–8.

Becker, G.S. (1983), 'A Theory of Competition Among Pressure Groups for Political Influence', *Quarterly Journal of Economics*, 47, 371–400.

Becker, G.S. (1985), 'Public Policies, Pressure Groups and Dead Weight Costs', *Journal of Political Economics*, 28, 329–47.

Berman, H. (1983), '*Law and Revolution: The Formation of the Western Legal Tradition*', Cambridge: Harvard University Press.

Bhagwati, J.N. (1980), 'Lobbying and Welfare', *Journal of Public Economics*, 14, 355–63.

Bhagwati, J.N., Brecher, R.A. and Srinivasan, T.N. (1984), 'DUP Activities and Economic Theory' in D.C. Colander (ed.), *Neoclassical Political Economy*, Cambridge: Ballinger, pp. 17–32.

Brady, G. and Tollison, R.D. (1991), 'Gordon Tullock: Creative Maverick of Public Choice', *Public Choice*, 71, 141–8.

Brennan, H.G. and Buchanan, J.M. (1980), *The Power to Tax: Analytical Foundations of a Fiscal Constitution*, London and New York: Cambridge University Press.

Browning, E.K. (1974), 'On the Welfare Costs of Transfers', *Kyklos*, 2, 374–7.

Buchanan, J.M. (1958), *Public Principles of Public Debt*, Homewood, IL: Irwin.

Buchanan, J.M. (1980a), 'Rent Seeking and Profit Seeking', in J.M. Buchanan, R.D. Tollison and G. Tullock (eds), *Toward a Theory of the Rent-Seeking Society*, College Station: Texas A. & M. University Press, pp. 3–15.

Buchanan, J.M. (1980b), 'Reform in the Rent-Seeking Society', in J.M. Buchanan, R.D. Tollison and G. Tullock (eds), *Toward a Theory of the Rent-Seeking Society*, College Station: Texas A. & M. University Press, pp. 359–67.

Buchanan, J.M., Rowley, C.K. and Tollison, R.D. (eds) (1987), *Deficits*, Oxford: Basil Blackwell.

Buchanan, J.M., Tollison, R.D. and Tullock, G. (eds) (1980), *Toward a Theory of the Rent-Seeking Society*, College Station: Texas A. & M. University Press.

Buchanan, J.M. and Tullock, G. (1962), *The Calculus of Consent: Logical Foundations of Constitutional Democracy*, Ann Arbor: University of Michigan Press.

Buchanan, J.M. and Wagner, R.E. (1977), *Democracy on Deficit: The Political Legacy of Lord Keynes*, New York: Academic Press.

Corcoran, W.J. (1984), 'Long-run Equilibrium and Total Expenditures in Rent-Seeking', *Public Choice*, 43, 89–94.

Corcoran, W.J. and Karels, G.U. (1985), 'Rent-Seeking Behavior in the Long-Run', *Public Choice*, 46, 227–46.

Crain, W.M. and Tollison, R.D. (1979), 'The Executive Branch in an Interest-Group Perspective', *Journal of Legal Studies*, 8, 555–67.

Crain, W.M. and Tollison, R.D. (1990), *Predicting Politics*, Ann Arbor: University of Michigan Press.

Crew, M.A. (1987), 'Rent-Seeking is Here to Stay', in C.K. Rowley (ed.), *Democracy and Public Choice: Essays in Honour of Gordon Tullock*', Oxford: Basil Blackwell.

Crew, M.A., Jones-Lee, M. and Rowley, C.K. (1971), 'X-Theory versus Management Discretion Theory', *Southern Economic Journal*, 37, 173–84.

Crew, M.A. and Rowley, C.K. (1971), 'On Allocative Efficiency, X-Efficiency and the Measurement of Welfare Loss', *Economica*, 38, 199–203.

Crew, M.A. and Rowley, C.K. (1988a), 'Toward a Public Choice Theory of Monopoly Regulation', *Public Choice*, 57, 49–68.

Crew, M.A. and Rowley, C.K. (1988b), 'Dispelling the Disinterest in Deregulation', in C.K. Rowley, R.D. Tollison and G.

Tullock (eds), *The Political Economy of Rent Seeking*, Boston: Kluwer Academic Publishers.

Downs, A. (1957), *An Economic Theory of Democracy*, New York: Harper and Row.

Downs, A. (1967), *Inside Bureaucracy*, Boston: Little Brown and Company.

Durden, G.C., Ellis, L.V. and Millsaps, S.W. (1991), 'Gordon Tullock: His Journal and His Scholarship', *Public Choice*, 71, 171–96.

Epstein, R.C. (1934), *Industrial Profits in the United States*, New York: National Bureau of Economic Research.

Fisher, F.M. (1985), 'The Social Costs of Monopoly and Regulation: Posner Reconsidered', *Journal of Political Economy*, 93, 410–16.

Franz, R. (1992), 'X-Efficiency and Allocative Efficiency: What Have We Learned?', *American Economic Review*, 82, 434–8.

Fukuyama, F. (1992), *The End of History and the Last Man*, New York: The Free Press.

Harberger, A.C. (1954), 'Monopoly and Resource Allocation', *American Economic Review*, 44, 77–87.

Harberger, A.C. (1959), 'Using the Resources at Hand More Effectively', *American Economic Review*, 49, 134–46.

Higgins, R.S., Shughart, W.F. and Tollison, R.D. (1985), 'Free Entry and Efficient Rent-Seeking', *Public Choice*, 46, 247–58.

Hillman, A.L. and Katz, E. (1984), 'Risk-Averse Rent-Seekers and the Social Cost of Monopoly Power', *Economic Journal*, 94, 104–10.

Hochman, H.M. and Rodgers, J.R. (1969), 'Pareto Optimal Redistribution', *American Economic Review*, 59, 542–57.

Johnson, H.G. (1958), 'The Gains from Freer Trade with Europe: An Estimate', *Manchester School of Economic and Social Studies*, 26, 247–55.

Krueger, A.O. (1974), 'The Political Economy of the Rent-Seeking Society', *American Economic Review*, 64, 291–303.

Laband, D.W. (forthcoming), 'An Estimate of Resource Expen-

Tullock, G. (1965b), *The Politics of Bureaucracy*, New York: University Press of America.

Tullock, G. (1966a), *The Organization of Inquiry*, Durham, NC: Duke University Press.

Tullock, G. (1966b), *Papers on Non-Market Decision Making I*, Charlottesville: Thomas Jefferson Center for Political Economy, University of Virginia.

Tullock, G. (1967a), *Towards a Mathematics of Politics*, Ann Arbor: University of Michigan.

Tullock, G. (1967b), 'The Welfare Costs of Tariffs, Monopolies and Theft', *Western Economic Journal*, 5, 224–32.

Tullock, G. (1971), 'The Cost of Transfers', *Kyklos*, 24, 629–43.

Tullock, G. (1974), 'More on the Welfare Cost of Transfers', *Kyklos*, 27, 378–81.

Tullock, G. (1975), 'Competing for Aid', *Public Choice*, 21, 41–52.

Tullock, G. (1980), 'Efficient Rent-Seeking', in J.M. Buchanan, R.D. Tollison and G. Tullock (eds), *Towards a Theory of the Rent-Seeking Society*, College Station: Texas A. & M. University Press.

Tullock, G. (1983), *The Economics of Income Redistribution*, Hingham, Mass: Kluwer-Nijhoff Publishing.

Tullock, G. (1985), 'Back to the Bog', *Public Choice*, 46, 259–63.

Tullock, G. (1987a), 'Another Part of the Swamp', *Public Choice*, 54, 83–4.

Tullock, G. (1987b), *Autocracy*, Boston: Kluwer Academic Publishers.

Tullock, G. (1988a), 'Efficient Rent-Seeking Revisited', in C.K. Rowley, R.D. Tollison and G. Tullock (eds), *The Political Economy of Rent-Seeking*, Boston: Kluwer Academic Publishers.

Tullock, G. (1988b), 'Rents and Rent-Seeking', in C.K. Rowley, R.D. Tollison and G. Tullock (eds), *The Political Economy of Rent-Seeking*, Boston: Kluwer Academic Publishers.

Tullock, G. (1988c), 'Future Directions for Rent-Seeking Research', in C.K. Rowley, R.D. Tollison and G. Tullock (eds),

ditures on Transfer Activity in the United States', *Quarterly Journal of Economics*, 58.

Laband, D.W. and Sophocleus, J.P. (1988), 'The Social Cost of Rent-Seeking: First Estimates', *Public Choice*, 58, 269–75.

Landes, W.M. and Posner, R.A. (1975), 'The Independent Judiciary in an Interest-Group Perspective', *Journal of Law and Economics*, 18, 875–901.

Leibenstein, H. (1966), 'Allocative Efficiency vs. X-Efficiency', *American Economic Review*, 56, 392–415.

McChesney, F.S. (1987), 'Rent Extraction and Rent Creation in the Theory of Economic Regulation', *Journal of Legal Studies*, 16, 101–18.

McChesney, F.S. (1991), 'Rent Extraction and Interest-Group Organization in a Coasean Model of Regulation', *Journal of Legal Studies*, 20, 73–90.

Magee, S.P., Brock, W.A. and Young, L. (1989), *Black Hole Tariffs and Endogenous Policy Theory*, Cambridge: Cambridge University Press.

Migue, P.L. and Bélanger, G. (1974), 'Toward a General Theory of Managerial Discretion', *Public Choice*, 17, 27–42.

Mitchell, W.C. and Munger, M.C. (1991), 'Economic Models of Interest Groups: An Introductory Survey', *American Journal of Political Science*, 35, 512–46.

Mundell, R.A. (1962), 'A Review of L.H. Janssen: Free Trade, Protection and Customs Unions', *American Economic Review*, 52, 622.

Murphy, K.M., Schleifer, A. and Vishny, R.W. (1990), *The Allocation of Talent: Implications for Growth*, University of Chicago manuscript.

Niskanen, W.A. (1971), *Bureaucracy and Representative Government*, Chicago: Aldine Press.

Niskanen, W.A. (1975), 'Bureaucrats and Politicians', *Journal of Law and Economics*, 18, 617–44.

North, D.C. (1990), *Institutions, Institutional Change and Economic Performance*, New York: Cambridge University Press.

Olson, M. (1965), *The Logic of Collective Action*, Cambridge: Harvard University Press.

Olson, M. (1982), *The Rise and Decline of Nations*, New Haven: Yale University Press.

Ostrom, V. (1984), 'Why Governments Fail: An Inquiry into the Use of Instruments of Evil to do Good', in J.M. Buchanan and R.D. Tollison (eds), *Theory of Public Choice, II*. Ann Arbor: University of Michigan Press, pp. 422–35.

Peacock, A.T. (1983), 'Public X-Inefficiency: International and Institutional Constraints', in H. Hanusch (ed.), *Anatomy of Government Deficiencies*, Heidelberg: Springer Verlag.

Peltzman, S. (1976), 'Towards a More General Theory of Regulation', *Journal of Law and Economics*, 19, 211–40.

Peltzman, S. (1990), 'How Efficient is the Voting Market?', *Journal of Law and Economics*, 33, 27–64.

Posner, R.A. (1975), 'The Social Costs of Monopoly and Regulation', *Journal of Political Economy*, 83, 807–27.

Rogerson, W.P. (1982), 'The Social Costs of Monopoly and Regulation: A Game-Theoretic Analysis', *Bell Journal of Economics and Management Science*, 13, 391–401.

Ross, V.B. (1984), '*Rent-Seeking in LDC Import Regimes: The Case of Kenya*', Geneva: Graduate Institute of International Studies, Papers in International Economics, No. 8408.

Rowley, C.K. (1973), *Antitrust and Economic Efficiency*, London: MacMillan.

Rowley, C.K. (1987), *Democracy and Public Choice: Essays in Honor of Gordon Tullock*, Oxford: Basil Blackwell.

Rowley, C.K. (1988a), 'Rent-Seeking Versus Directly Unproductive Profit-Seeking Activities', in C.K. Rowley, R.D. Tollison and G. Tullock (eds), *The Political Economy of Rent-Seeking*, Boston: Kluwer Academic Publishing.

Rowley, C.K. (1988b), 'Rent-Seeking in Constitutional Perspective', in C.K. Rowley, R.D. Tollison and G. Tullock (eds), *The Political Economy of Rent-Seeking*, Boston: Kluwer Academic Publishers, pp. 447–64.

Rowley, C.K. (1991), 'Gordon Tullock: Entrepreneur of Public Choice', *Public Choice*, 71, 149–70.

Rowley, C.K. (1992a), *The Right to Justice: The Political*

Economy of Legal Services in the United States, Brookfield, Vermont and Aldershot, England: Edward Elgar Publishing.

Rowley, C.K. (1992b), 'The Supreme Court and Takings Judgements: Constitutional Political Economy versus Public Choice', in N. Mercuro (ed.), *Taking Property and Just Compensation: Law and Economics Perspectives of the Takings Issue*, Boston: Kluwer Academic Publishers, pp. 79–124.

Rowley, C.K. and Elgin, R.S. (1985), 'Toward a Theory of Bureaucratic Behaviour', in D. Greenaway and G.K. Shaw (eds), *Public Choice, Public Finance and Public Policy*, Oxford: Basil Blackwell, pp. 31–50.

Rowley, C.K., Shughart, W.F. and Tollison, R.D. (1987), 'Interest Groups and Deficits', in J.M. Buchanan, C.K. Rowley and R.D. Tollison (eds), *Deficits*, Oxford: Basil Blackwell, pp. 263–80.

Rowley, C.K. and Tollison, R.D. (1986), 'Rent-Seeking and Trade Protection', *Swiss Journal of International Relations*, 141–66.

Rowley, C.K., Tollison, R.D. and Tullock, G. (eds) (1988), *The Political Economy of Rent-Seeking*, Boston: Kluwer Academic Publishers.

Rowley, C.K. and Tullock, G. (1988), 'Introduction' in C.K. Rowley, R.D. Tollison and G. Tullock (eds), *The Political Economy of Rent-Seeking*, Boston: Kluwer Academic Publishers, 3–14.

Schwartzman, D. (1960), 'The Burden of Monopoly', *Journal of Political Economy*, 68, 727–9.

Stigler, G.J. (1971), 'The Theory of Economic Regulation', *Bell Journal of Economics and Management Science*, 2, 3–21.

Stigler, G.J. (1974), 'Free Riders and Collective Action: An Appendix to Theories of Economic Regulation', *Bell Journal of Economics and Management Science*, 5, 359–65.

Stigler, G.J. (1976), 'Xistence of X-efficiency?', *American Economic Review*, 66, 213–16.

Tullock, G. (1959), 'Some Problems of Majority Voting', *Journal of Political Economy*, 67, 571–9.

Tullock, G. (1965a), 'Constitutional Mythology', *New Individualist Review*, 3, 13–17.

The Political Economy of Rent-Seeking, Boston: Kluwer Academic Publishers.

Tullock, G. (1989), *The Economics of Special Privilege and Rent-Seeking*, Boston: Kluwer Academic Publishers.

Wagner, R.E. (1966), 'Price Groups and Political Entrepreneurs: A Review Article', *Papers on Non-Market Decision-Making*, 1, 161–70.

Wagner, R.E. (1987), 'Parchment, Guns and the Maintenance of Constitutional Contract', in C.K. Rowley (ed.), *Democracy and Public Choice: Essays in Honor of Gordon Tullock*, Oxford: Basil Blackwell, pp. 105–21.

Wagner, R.E. (1988), 'Agency, Economic Calculation and Constitutional Construction', in C.K. Rowley, R.D. Tollison and G. Tullock (eds), *The Political Economy of Rent-Seeking*, Boston: Kluwer Academic Publishers, pp. 423–46.

Warren, C. (1922), *The Supreme Court in United States History*: Vol. I, Boston: Little Brown.

Watson, D.S. (1965), *Price Theory in Action: A Book of Readings*, New York: Houghton Mifflin Company.

Watson, D.S. (1968), *Price Theory in Action*, Boston: Houghton Mifflin Company.

Weingast, B.R. and Moran, M.J. (1983), 'Bureaucratic Discretion or Congressional Control: Regulatory Policy Making by the Federal Trade Commission', *Journal of Political Economy*, 91, 765–800.

Wemelsfelder, J. (1960), 'The Short-Term Effect of Lowering Import Duties in Germany', *Economic Journal*, 60, 94–104.

Index